KT-408-937

BARCELONA

CONDENSED

barcelona-tourist-guide.com

 martin hughes

LONELY PLANET PUBLICATIONS
Melbourne • Oakland • London • Paris

contents

Barcelona Condensed
1st edition – May 2002

Published by
Lonely Planet Publications Pty Ltd
ABN 36 005 607 983
90 Maribyrnong St, Footscray, Vic 3011, Australia
www.lonelyplanet.com or AOL keyword: lp

Lonely Planet offices
Australia Locked Bag 1, Footscray, Vic 3011
           ☎ 03-8379 8000 fax 03-8379 81
           e talk2us@lonelyplanet.com.au
USA   150 Linden St, Oakland, CA 94607
           ☎ 510-893 8555 Toll Free: 800 275 8555
           fax 510-893 8572
           e info@lonelyplanet.com
UK   10a Spring Place, London NW5 3BH
           ☎ 020-7428 4800 fax 020-7428 4828
           e go@lonelyplanet.co.uk
France   1 rue du Dahomey, 75011 Paris
           ☎ 01 55 25 33 00 fax 01 55 25 33 01
           e bip@lonelyplanet.fr
           www.lonelyplanet.fr

Cover Jenny Jones Editing Imogen Franks & Bridget
Blair Design James Ellis Maps Alison Lyall, Charles
Rawlings-Way & Sophie Reed Proofing Charlie Beech
& Michala Green Publishing Manager Diana Saad
Thanks to Annie Horner, Gabrielle Green, James Hardy,
Quentin Frayne, Sam Trafford, Rowan McKinnon, Ryan
Evans, Tim Ryder and especially to Martin.

Photographs
Many of the images in this guide are available for
licensing from Lonely Planet Images:
www.lonelyplanetimages.com

Front cover photographs
Top Passion facade towers, La Sagrada Familia
(Dale Buckton)
Bottom La Pedrera
(Jenny J Jones)

ISBN 1 74059 335 9

Text & maps © Lonely Planet Publications Pty Ltd 2002
Barcelona metro map: grateful acknowledgement is
made for reproduction permission © TMB Barcelona
City Map 2002
Photos © photographers as indicated 2002
Printed through Colorcraft Ltd, Hong Kong
Printed in China

All rights reserved. No part of this publication may
be reproduced, stored in a retrieval system or
transmitted in any form by any means, electronic,
mechanical, photocopying, recording or otherwise,
except brief extracts for the purpose of review,
without the written permission of the publisher.
Lonely Planet, the Lonely Planet logo, Lonely Planet
Images, CitySync and eKno are trade marks of Lonely
Planet Publications Pty Ltd. Other trade marks are
the property of their respective owners.

Although the authors and Lonely Planet try to make the
information as accurate as possible, we accept no
responsibility for any loss, injury or inconvenience
sustained by anyone using this book.

Martin Hughes

how to use this book

SYMBOLS

⊠ address

☎ telephone number

Ⓜ nearest metro station

🚇 nearest train station

🚌 nearest bus route

🚕 taxi/driving options

🕓 opening hours

ⓘ tourist information

Ⓢ cost, entry charge

ⓔ email/Web site address

♿ wheelchair access

⚲ child-friendly

✗ on-site or nearby eatery

Ⓥ good vegetarian selection

COLOUR-CODING

Each chapter has a different colour code, which is reflected on the maps for quick reference (eg, all Highlights are bright yellow on the maps).

MAPS

The fold-out maps on the inside front and back covers are numbered from 1 to 7. All sights and venues in the text have map references that indicate where to find them on the maps; eg, (3, E6) means Map 3, grid reference E6. Although each item is not pin-pointed on the maps, the street address is always indicated.

PRICES

Price gradings (eg, €10/5) usually indicate adult/concession admission charges to a venue. Concession prices can include child, senior and student discounts.

AUTHOR AUTHOR!

Martin Hughes

Martin was born and bred in Dublin where, as an adult, he dithered for five years between journalism and public relations. He caught the travel bug after a two-week holiday in Barcelona and wandered for three years through Europe, Asia and Australia avoiding a cure. He settled in Melbourne, Australia, and helped set up Lonely Planet's World Food series, for which he wrote two titles. He returns to Barcelona every couple of years to shake the dirt off his roots.

Thanks to Kirsti, Andrea, Cam, Shukri, Agostino, Alex, Sara, Emma, Imogen, and Damien Simonis for a terrific first draft.

READER FEEDBACK

Things change – prices go up, schedules change, good places go bad and bad places improve or go bankrupt. So, if you find things better or worse, recently opened or long since closed, please tell us and help make the next edition even more accurate. Send all correspondence to the Lonely Planet office closest to you (listed on p. 2) or visit www.lonelyplanet.com/feedback.

Lonely Planet books provide independent advice. Lonely Planet does not accept advertising in guidebooks, nor payment in exchange for listing or endorsing any place or business. Lonely Planet writers do not accept discounts or payments in exchange for positive coverage of any sort.

facts about barcelona

When Franco died in 1975, all the creative energy that had been bottled up under the reviled dictator was suddenly unleashed. Over the following decades Barcelona transformed from a smug Mediterranean backwater into one of the hippest and most stylish capitals of the world. The city is now a model for others trying to keep their identity intact amid the maelstrom of globalisation. While it cuts a splendid dash on the international stage and welcomes allcomers, it is fortifying Catalan heritage by fiercely protecting and promoting its independent spirit.

And what qualities to brag about! It is an economic powerhouse and a city that rarely sleeps. Its people work and play with such feverish intensity that it's a toss up whether they are insanely serious or seriously insane. From Gothic to Gaudí, the architecture will make you swoon. World-class museums will nourish your soul and the cuisine will make your palate spin. But more than the cultural treasures of yesteryear, it's the vitality of the present that makes Barcelona so appealing. The

creative energy continues to fizz – in music, art, architecture, fashion and sport. It might not have any more qualities than other major cities but no place on earth puts them together with such pizzazz.

It's a mind-blowing cocktail, made with equal measures of culture, style and passion, and with a dash of petty street crime to give it some zest. It is unimaginable until you arrive, unbelievable while you are here and unforgettable after you've left – that's if you ever leave.

Whether rambling, dancing, prancing or romancing, Barcelona is a city for all ages.

HISTORY
Early Barcelona
It wasn't until the Romans established Barcino in the 3rd century BC that the city really began to emerge. After short visits by the Visigoths and the Moors, it was taken over by the Franks in the 7th century AD.

The Call
Street names to the east of the Generalitat (4, E7) featuring the word 'call' (from Hebrew for 'meeting place') reveal that this was once a Jewish ghetto, founded in the second century. Despite having its fortunes decided by the vicissitudes of power and recurring anti-Semitism, the Call became a renowned centre of learning by the 11th century. It generated great envy and, in 1391, was sacked in a wave of pogroms, sparked by rumours that the Jews had brought the Black Death. The community never recovered and the few Jews who remained were expelled from the area in 1424.

Martin Hughes

Barcelona's Counts
A local man, Guifré el Pelós (Wilfred the Hairy) gained control over several territories and the Frankish king made him the first count of Barcelona. He founded a dynasty that lasted for almost five centuries and is remembered as the 'father of Catalunya'.

The Golden Age
After a tiff with the Franks, Catalunya declared itself autonomous. Through marriage the region then joined with the Crown of Aragon, which enabled it to expand an empire that stretched across the Mediterranean in what is known as the Catalan 'golden age'.

Castilian Dominance
Overstretched, racked by civil disobedience and decimated by the Black Death, Catalunya began to wobble by the 14th century. When the last count of Wilfred the Hairy's dynasty died without an heir, the Crown of Aragon was passed to a member of the Castilian nobility. Soon these two Spanish kingdoms were united and Catalunya was left on the outer. As business shifted from the Mediterranean to the Atlantic with the discovery of the Americas, Catalans were banned from trade and Castile boomed while Catalunya went bust.

The region was further weakened by two major revolts over the next century. The Reapers' War of 1640, sparked when peasant farmers murdered the viceroy, eventually saw it lose the territory north of the Pyrenees to France. It backed the wrong side in the War of the Spanish Succession (1702-13) and paid the price when the eventual king, Felipe V, established a unitary Castilian state. He banned the writing and teaching of Catalan, and built a huge fort (now Parc de la Ciutadella) to watch over Barcelona's troublemakers.

Economic Growth & the Renaixença

Buoyed by the lifting of the ban on trade with the Americas in 1778, Catalunya launched one of the first industrial revolutions in Europe. As the economy prospered, Barcelona outgrew its medieval walls, which were demolished in 1854. Work on l'Eixample (the Extension) began soon after.

The 1888 Universal Exhibition gave Barcelona the impetus to transform itself into a modern city and propelled the Renaixença (Renaissance), a movement dedicated to the revival of the Catalan language and culture.

Anarchy

However, the relative prosperity brought little improvement to the lives of the workers and, at the turn of the 20th century, violence among the various factions looking for a bigger piece of the pie was commonplace.

Spain's neutrality during WWI boosted its economy and within 20 years Barcelona had doubled in size. Workers wages, meanwhile, were devalued following the associated rise in inflation. During a wave of general strikes, organised principally by the anarchists Confederación Nacional del Trabajo (CNT), employers hired hit men to eliminate the union leaders. More than 800 people were killed within five years. It took the International Exhibition of 1929 to stimulate Barcelona's economy again.

Revival of Catalan Nationalism & the Spanish Civil War

The Second Spanish Republic was established in 1931, after which a power struggle between Republicans (an uneasy coalition of leftist parties) and Nationalists (an alliance of the army, church and fascists) took a grip on Spain. Franco-led nationalists in the army rose against the government and sparked the Spanish Civil War, which lasted from 1936 to 1939, the year a battered Barcelona finally fell to Franco.

The Franco Era

Franco was reviled in Catalunya and the first two decades of his reign were one of the bleakest periods in Barcelona's modern history. All things Catalan were suppressed, the city was overcrowded and impoverished, and anyone who didn't tow the line was brutally punished.

It wasn't until the late 1950s that Barcelona regained the standard of living it had enjoyed pre-Franco. When he died in 1975, the city rejoiced. Two years later, Catalunya was once again granted regional autonomy. All the creative energy that had been bottled up in the preceding decades popped like so many bottles of cava. From fashion to architecture and business to the arts, the city fizzed. The 1992 Olympics allowed Barcelona to once again strut its stuff on the world stage, projecting an image of cultural prosperity. It hasn't looked back since.

ORIENTATION

Barcelona is remarkably compact, occupying a plain between an amphi-
theatre of hills and the Mediterranean. Bounding the city on its landward
side is Tibidabo, the highest peak of the range and pedestal for a church,
Temple del Sagrat Cor, that you can see from most of the city. This guide
concentrates on an inverted 'T', with the horizontal line running along the
coast from the hill of Montjuïc in the southwest to Barceloneta and Port
Olímpic in the northeast. La Rambla runs perpendicular to the coastline,
and has the medieval areas of Barri Gòtic and La Ribera to its west and El
Raval to its east. Heading away
from the coast, La Rambla leads to
Plaça Catalunya, which marks the
boundary between Barcelona's old
and new quarters. Pg de Gràcia
continues the (more or less) straight
line and is the main artery of
l'Eixample (the Extension), which
connects with Gracia, another
medieval area that was once a separate village from the city.

El Quatre Barres

Catalunya's flag – four red stripes on a
gold background – is said to represent
the four bloody fingers drawn by the
mortally wounded Wilfred the Hairy
across his shield as he lay dying on the
battlefield. It is believed to be the oldest national flag in Europe.

Martin Hughes

The use of both Catalan and
Castilian in street names can be
confusing to the unsuspecting vis-
itor. In this guide the following
abbreviations have been used:
Avda for Avinguda/Avenida, Bda
for Baixada/Bajada, C/ for Carrer/
Calle and Pg for Passeig/Paseo.

ENVIRONMENT

While Barcelona isn't spared the air pollution common among crowded
Mediterranean conurbations, you won't find it overwhelmingly uncomfortable. The (virtually) traffic-free old quarters are where visitors most
like to roam anyway. If the smog or fumes start getting you down, simply
head to the beach or the hilltops to clean out your lungs. The beaches
aren't paradise, but they are fine for a dip and can guarantee you fresh sea
air.

Your biggest discomfort will probably be the stench of piss along
many streets of the old quarters, which seem to double as popular public
urinals. Along with the lackadaisical attitude to garbage disposal and
piles of poochy poo, the medieval streets won't always provide the romantic setting you had in mind. The streets – and occasionally careless revellers
– are thoroughly hosed down every night but it seems to make little
difference.

Noise pollution is another by-product of Barcelona's appeal and can also
be a hindrance to happy holidays. See p. 102 for more details.

GOVERNMENT & POLITICS

The Generalitat de Catalunya, the region's autonomous parliament, was resurrected by royal decree in 1977. It has wide powers over matters such as education, health, trade, industry, tourism and agriculture, and is housed in the Palau de la Generalitat (6, D3) on Plaça de Sant Jaume. Facing it across the same square is the Ajuntament (city council), which is responsible for tourism, public transport, the arts and social security in Barcelona. Neither is seriously pushing for Catalan independence. Indeed, less than 10% of the electorate pursue the notion with their vote and there is no Catalan equivalent of the Basque terror group, ETA.

A third, anonymous political force occupies a building next to the Estació de França in La Ribera. The unelected Delegaciòn del Gobierno takes its orders direct from Madrid and keeps an eye on the chaps over on Plaça de Sant Jaume.

Meanwhile, the spirit of anarchy remains strong on the streets and a World Bank Forum, due to be held in the city in 2001, had to be cancelled due to security concerns.

> **Did You Know?**
> - There are two official languages in barcelona: Catalan, the language of the region, and Castilian (or Spanish), the official language of the country.
> - Greater Barcelona's population is 3 million.
> - Unemployment stands at 6% in Catalunya.

Crest on the Palau de la Generalitat

ECONOMY

Barcelona, the chief commercial and industrial centre of Spain, has a reputation for being a hard-working and a mercantile city. The roots of its trading culture lie in the days of Mediterranean empire building, but industry first stirred to life in the small-scale textiles factories that emerged late in the 18th century and helped to propel the industrial revolution. The city grew prosperous on metallurgy and engineering during the 19th century.

Today, it's an economic powerhouse. Almost 25% of all Spanish exports come from Catalunya (mainly in and around Barcelona). Textiles and other manufacturing industries are big business, along with international banking, finance and tourism. The latter is a major industry with more than 3.5 million visitors, double the number before the 1992 Olympics, flocking to the port city each year.

Unemployment is low by European standards. Although inflation is on the rise, and the cost of living is more of a problem here than elsewhere in Spain, the analysts are optimistic.

SOCIETY & CULTURE

Considering the number of tourists that swamp Barcelona, its people are extraordinarily tolerant and courteous. Where else would you get a muscle-bound, tattoo-covered truck driver who would rather hold up traffic than spoil your holiday snap?

People do not expect you to speak Catalan although they will warm to you much quicker if you can tickle their ears with a word or two. Even if you good-humouredly fumble your way through *castellano* (Castilian or Spanish), they'll bend over backwards to help you. One thing sure to annoy a Catalan is assuming that they speak English. Learn a few basic phrases.

The influx of immigrants from poorer parts of Spain during the mid-20th century broadened the social make-up of the city. However, you'll generally get along better with everyone if you get into the habit of referring to 'Catalunya' rather than 'Spain'.

Most of the city's 1.5 million residents are Catholic although many Barcelonins pay little more than lip service to their faith.

Etiquette

Barcelonins aren't as hung up as Anglos tend to be with the niceties of social intercourse. Excesses of *'por favors'* (please) and *'gracias'* (thank you) are not the norm and even the friendliest people will simply say 'give me ... (whatever)'. If somebody thanks you, *'de nada'* (it's nothing) is the most polite response and you can get a waiter's attention by calling *'oiga'* (hear me).

When entering a shop or a bar, it is customary to wish all and sundry a hearty *'hola'* and to bid them *'adiós'* when you leave.

Men and women and women with women, even when they meet for the first time, greet each other with a glancing kiss on each cheek, right then left. Outside business, men don't seem too fussed about handshakes with other men but it's always good to offer.

Ladies needn't return home with tans spoiled by bikini-top lines – it's perfectly acceptable to get your boobs out at the beach.

Smokers can puff to their heart's content pretty much anywhere (as the locals do).

Do as the locals: relax and soak up the atmosphere (or the beer).

ARTS
Architecture

Think of architecture and Barcelona, and it's usually Gaudí who springs to mind. But if one word best described the city's architectural heritage, it would more likely be Gothic. Barcelona is one of Europe's great Gothic treasure chests and it was largely from this reservoir of riches that the Modernistas of the late 19th and early 20th centuries supped so keenly, adapting the old to fit their new ways of seeing and building.

Besides some impressive left-overs of Roman walls and a precious few Romanesque highlights, Barcelona's architectural personality begins with its version of the Gothic style that emerged in Europe in the 13th century. Catalan Gothic reflected the confidence and innovation of Catalunya during its golden age of expansion and took its own unique course. Decoration was used more sparingly than elsewhere but, most significantly, the Catalan builders championed breadth over height. Stunning examples of Catalan Gothic can be found in the Palau Reial's Saló del Tinell, Drassanes (the former shipyards that are now home to the Museu Marítim) and the church of Santa Maria del Mar.

Modernisme emerged as a trend throughout the arts in Barcelona during the 1880s, the city's *belle époque*. While the name suggests a rejection of the old, the pioneers of the style actually delved deeply into the past for inspiration, absorbed it all and then ripped up the rulebook. They even used many traditional materials, albeit applying them in a thoroughly innovative way. Although aligned to the Art Nouveau and Jugendstil styles in France and Germany a little later, Modernisme was more vigorous, bold and playful, and had a character all of its own.

Reclaiming Gaudí

You'll soon realise that the reputation of Gaudí (Catalan for 'delight') plays a large part in fuelling Barcelona's tourism industry and the locals are proud as punch of his flamboyant feats. Yet, for the latter part of his career and right up until the 1960s, he was thought eccentric and irrelevant. His reputation has undergone such a transformation that he is now officially in line for beatification from the Vatican and the canny folk of Barcelona designated 2002 (the 150th anniversary of his birth) to be International Gaudí Year, with special exhibitions and events organised in Barcelona and all over the world.

Martin Hughes

Architecture was the most visible aspect of the movement, today synonymous with the name Antonio Gaudí. He personifies (and in large measure transcends) the thunderclap of innovative greatness that helped transform an otherwise middle-ranking (artistically speaking) European city into a modern capital. While Gaudí's works are the most well known examples, Lluís Domènech i Montaner is regarded as the original and Josep Puig i Cadafalch completes the trio of great Modernistas. But the style may not have emerged – or have been so successful, at least – if it hadn't been for the extraordinary skills of the artisans and craftspeople who worked with the architects to create these astonishing works.

Painting

While there might not be much Romanesque architecture still standing in Barcelona, the city has the world's best collection of paintings from the period. A great many anonymous artists left their work behind in the chapels and churches of medieval Catalunya, mostly in the form of murals and altarpieces, which depicted religious figures with an other-worldly awe. Much of this work was salvaged and can be seen today in the Museu Nacional d'Art de Catalunya (MNAC; p. 26), which also exhibits the sombrely realistic style of Gothic art that followed.

Ramòn Casas was the most famous artist to emerge from the Modernisme period in Barcelona but he was soon to be overshadowed by the true genius of Pablo Picasso. Born in Màlaga in 1881, Picasso spent many of his teenage years in Barcelona in the company of the Modernistas. By the time he moved to Paris in 1904, he had already explored his first personal style in the so-called Blue Period. He went on to create cubism and become the greatest artist of the 20th century but he always retained a soft spot for Catalunya.

Continuing the burst of brilliance was the surrealist Joan Miró (1893-1983), who is best remembered for his use of symbolic figures in primary colours. Hot on his heels was the most famous surrealist of all, Salvador Dalí, who spent precious little time in Barcelona but deserves a mention because his monument to his own nuttiness, the Teatre-Museu Dalí, is merely an excursion away. Antoni Tàpies (born 1923) is the most important contemporary artist in Barcelona today and highly regarded in Spain.

If you like Joan Miró, sit down...

Martin Hughes

highlights

Between museums that boggle with their brilliance and buildings that confound with their creativity, Barcelona has enough sights to keep you exploring for months. The highlights listed here are a combination of old favourites and ones that you really shouldn't miss. Most of the major attractions are clustered closely together within easy walking distance of one another and the few that require legwork are genuinely worth the effort. See p. 35 for information on discount passes.

Stopping Over?

One Day Take the city's pulse with a ramble along La Rambla and refreshments at any of its overpriced cafes. Wander through the medieval marvel of the Barri Gòtic to Museu Picasso in La Ribera, before retiring to lunch around the church of Santa Maria del Mar. Refuelled, catch the metro to La Sagrada Família and enter a trance as you climb its towers. After a sunset stroll along the promenade of Port Olímpic, return to La Ribera for tapas, before making a beeline for El Borne.

Two Days Start off with the Modernista masterpieces of Pg de Gràcia, taking in Gaudí's La Pedrera and the Manzana de la Discordia. Enjoy an alfresco meal on the palatial Rambla de Catalunya and browse in its boutiques. Stroll down towards the old quarter and book yourself in for a tour of the wonderful Palau de la Música Catalana before heading up the mountain of Montjuïc to admire the works of a gifted Catalan at the Fundación Joan Miró. Follow dinner with a bar crawl through the Barri Gòtic.

Three Days Amble through the Barri Gòtic and the Catedral, where you can take a lift to the roof and splendid views. Tour the nearby underground remains of the Roman city at the Museu d'Història de la Ciutat and explore the rooms of the former royal palace. Giddy-up to Gaudí's Parc Güell and, after a relaxing couple of hours, head to Plaça del Sol in Gràcia and let the night take over.

Barcelona Lowlights

Here's a subjective list of things you're least likely to find in the tourist brochures. You may be able to handle these, but they don't ring our bell.

- The constant warnings about pick pockets and the probability of it happening to you
- The stench of urine throughout most of the old quarters
- Noisy hotel rooms – if the traffic or revellers don't get you, the barking dogs will
- Most of the new development on Port Vell
- Having to book hotel rooms way in advance
- The noisy, polluted Via Laietana, which divides Barri Gòtic and La Ribera

Read all about it

Martin Hughes

BARÇA (2, G3)

Barcelona Football Club embodies the spirit of Catalunya. One of Europe's biggest (and wealthiest) clubs, it is magnificently housed in the **Nou Camp** (officially called Camp Nou) stadium, one of the world's largest football arenas and hallowed turf for any fan of the game. Although Barça's trophy room shows it has underachieved as a team – rivals Real Madrid eclipse its successes, even in Spain – this club can't be beaten for colour, character, big names and passion.

It was founded (ironically, by non-Catalans) in 1899 and has been at the highest echelon of Spanish football ever since. Despite its nationalist rhetoric, its links with foreigners have been strong and in recent years the team has largely comprised of outrageously paid foreign mercenaries (ie, the cream of international football). Fans still mourn the passing – to fierce rivals, Real Madrid, so he may as well be dead – a few years back of Portuguese genius, Luis Figo.

The city's second team is Espanyol, which has been going for almost as long but without anywhere near the success or profile. Because of Barça's superiority on the pitch, rivalry between the two clubs is more political than skilful, with Espanyol seen as more Spanish than Catalan. The fact that Espanyol usually has more Catalans in its team matters little.

INFORMATION

- ✉ Avda Arstides Maillol
- ☎ 93 496 36 00
- e www.fcbarcelona.com
- Ⓜ Maria Cristina or Collblanc
- ⊘ info & tickets: Mon-Fri 9.30am-1.30pm & 4.30-7.30pm; museum: Mon-Sat 10.30am-6.30pm, Sun 10am-2pm
- ⑤ match tickets: €20-90; museum: €3.40/2.20
- ⓘ tickets also on sale through Servi-Caixa (see p. 87)
- ♿ good
- ✗ cafe

Martin Hughes

If you're a sports fan, getting a ticket for one of Nou Camp's 120,000 seats to watch a game will probably be a priority. It can be simple or nigh-on impossible, depending on the match and your means. Five-star hotels keep season tickets – excellent seats – for guests' use. Otherwise, you can queue up outside the stadium a week before the match, buy from touts, or go into any branch of La Caixa bank (see p. 87) where you'll have no problem buying a ticket for one of the smaller games. The Nou Camp is an unforgettable experience when

Footie ain't forbidden in the Nou Camp!

the opposition is good enough to fire up the home crowd. For lesser matches, it might be relatively calm compared to what you're used to; the fans are a respectable cross-section of society and while the atmosphere is always electric it doesn't necessarily crackle.

If you can't get to a match, the **Museu del Futbol Club Barcelona** will provide some consolation (and a view of the stadium). Astonishingly, it is the city's most popular museum – yes, more popular than the Museu Picasso – and is normally as crowded as the six-yard box for a corner. The crowds are made up of football fanatics, tolerant partners and coachloads of packaged tourists who just heard it was popular. Despite the volumes of people, it maintains the hushed reverence of a cathedral.

Dragged-along partners will find it surprisingly charming – perhaps more so than the dragging fanatics. On display are stacks of old photographs, mementos, models, sculptures, posters, programmes, jerseys, boots and balls. Pride of place in the trophy cabinet is the 1992 European Cup and a monitor nearby plays the final on continuous loop. But, to be honest, when it's not your own team, it can all get a bit ho-hum.

Downstairs, there is a huge store selling Barcelona FC merchandise, the highlight of which is an enormously tacky stall that will provide a photograph of you wearing the Barça colours and scoring a goal in the Nou Camp with Patrick Kluivert (or whoever you like) racing up to congratulate you. And they don't offer a discount when you buy in bulk.

Bums Behind Barça

Unusually for such a big football club, Barcelona FC is owned by the fans, or the *culés* (bums) as they are affectionately known. They got the delightful nickname from people who used to pass the stadium and see row upon row of posteriors hanging over the perimeter wall.

Martin Hughes

Young habits die hard.

CATEDRAL (4, D8)

Soaring above the Barri Gòtic, Barcelona's central place of worship presents a magnificent image. It is a towering monument to more than 1500 years of continuous Catalan worship and the third church to be built on what was once the heart of the Roman forum.

INFORMATION

✉ Plaça de la Seu
Ⓜ Jaume I
🕐 8.30am-1.30pm & 4-7.30pm (reopens at 5pm weekends); lift to the roof Mon-Sat 10.30am-12.30pm & 4.30-6.30pm
💲 €1.20 for lift
♿ good
✕ see p. 74-9

Martin Hughes

Martin Lladó

The only way is up... but there is a lift.

The imposing, decorative facade was only added in the late 19th century (albeit to 15th-century design), while the rest of the Catedral was built from 1298 to 1460. The interior is immense, divided into a central nave and two aisles by lines of slim, elegant pillars. One of the few churches spared from the arson attacks of anarchists, its grandiose and, at times heavy-handed, ornamentation remains intact.

Inside the main entrance to your left is a baptistry, where the six Native Americans brought back by Columbus in 1493 as souvenirs and proof of his discoveries were baptised. Smack in the middle of the central nave are the 14th-century choir stalls, which face the crypt of Santa Eulàlia, one of Barcelona's two patron saints. Beside them is a lift that will take you to the roof of the church and breathtaking views.

With all the Eucharistic goings-on and the confessional whisperings, the scrupulously pious tone of this place can become overbearing. Through a Romanesque door (the only surviving remnant from the Catedral's 11th-century predecessor) you can head out into a lovely cloister. The honking geese around the fountain have been here since time immemorial and are possibly descendants of Roman birds.

DON'T MISS
- Sant Crist de Lepant, the lucky crucifix borne by Don Juan's flagship into battle at Lepanto • the Romanesque chapel of Santa Llúcia • Pere Sanglada's carvings on the pulpit

FUNDACIÓN JOAN MIRÓ (1, A4)

Forever leaving a piece of himself in his native Barcelona, Joan Miró established this gallery on the hill of Montjuïc in 1971. The largest single collection of his work is housed here, in a magnificent building designed by his friend Josep Lluís Sert. The combination of natural light, white walls and airy galleries make this a wonderful setting to appreciate the works of Catalunya's greatest artist.

Miró, although principally a painter, dabbled in every medium he could get his hands on and the museum houses sculptures, engravings, lithographs and ceramics, plus a huge legacy of drawings and other work, as well as more than 300 paintings. Only a small part of the collection can be displayed at any one time but still there is always far too much to take in on just one visit.

The permanent exhibition tends to concentrate on Miró's more settled final years, but it also gives captivating insights into the evolution of his work and traces the changes in his style and rebelliousness to conventional painting. Many of the works reflect his trademark delicate, yet aggressive, use of primary colours and symbols, while others convey his wit and sense of the absurd. There are also many wonderful sculptures in and around the building, by Miró and others, and one room contains paintings donated by other artists after Miró's death in 1983.

The fundación is much more than just a place to house Miró's work, however – it also hosts impressive temporary shows, exhibits the work of young contemporary artists in its basement and has a terrific public library.

INFORMATION

- ✉ Parc de Montjuïc
- ☎ 93 329 19 08
- e www.bcn.fjmiro.es
- Ⓜ Paral.lel, then Funicular de Montjuïc
- ◷ Tues-Sat 10am-7pm (to 9.30pm Thur, to 8pm in summer), Sun 10am-2.30pm
- Ⓢ €7.20/4
- ♿ excellent
- ✗ take a picnic

Martin Hughes

Martin Hughes

Are you looking at me?

DON'T MISS
- Miró's *Man and Woman in Front of a Pile of Excrement* (1935)
- Miró's sculpture *The Ladder of the Evading Eye* (1971) • Alexander Calder's *Mercury Fountain* (1937)

GRÀCIA (5)

Once a separate village north of Barcelona, Gràcia has long been renowned as a crucible for liberal attitudes and Catalan nationalism. When l'Eixample was built, the area was absorbed by the city, to the chagrin of many locals. You'll still see sarcastic slogans calling for Gràcia's independence. In the 1970s, when lots of groovy bars and restaurants sprung up on its narrow, atmospheric streets and sociable plaças, it was the hippest quarter of the metropolis, Today, it is a laid-back Bohemian haven, a million miles (well, a couple of metro stops) from the posturing of Barcelona, and gloriously free from tourists.

INFORMATION

- Ⓜ Fontana or Diagonal
- ⓘ most lively on weekend evenings
- ✕ see p. 85

Pascale Beroujon
The sun shines on Gràcia's Plaça del Sol.

It still clings steadfastly to its character and hosts Barcelona's most exuberant *festa major* (festival) for a few days in late August when the precinct pulsates to around-the-clock partying and thousands of visiting Barcelonins are tolerated for the sake of the festa.

The most atmospheric part of Gràcia is the area surrounding Fontana metro station (5, B1) where you'll find the **Mercat de la Llibertat**, the Modernista roof of which was built by Francesc Berenguer i Mestres, Gràcia's de facto architect. Berenguer, as well as being Gaudí's assistant and foreman (his 'own right arm'), built many attractive residences here. You can see several of them on Gran de Gràcia, most notably Casa Cama (built 1905) at No 15. Because he never completed architecture school – leaving at 21 to marry and have seven children – Berenguer was seldom credited for his works, in the official records at least.

DON'T MISS
- alfresco dining on Plaça del Sol • Gaudí's Casa Vicenç at C/de les Carolines 18-24 • Las Guitarras bar • Berenguer's Casa Rubina at C/de l'Or 44

LA PEDRERA   (5, G2)

The most extraordinary apartment block ever built was originally called Casa Milà – after its owner – but was nicknamed La Pedrera (The Stone Quarry) by befuddled locals who watched Antoni Gaudí build it from 1905 to 1910. Its rippling grey stone facade looks more like a cliff face sculpted by waves and wind than something made by man, and is studded with seaweed in the form of wrought-iron balconies.

On the fourth floor you can visit a recreated Modernista apartment, **El Pis de la Pedrera**, furnished in the style a prosperous family might have enjoyed when the block was completed. No two apartments are the same but this one – with its sensuous curves and stylish little touches – is filled with antiques from the era and makes for a fascinating wander.

Espai Gaudí (Gaudí Space) is housed in what used to be the attic and feels like the building's rib cage. It now offers a thorough overview of Gaudí's work and methods, and screens a wonderful visual display of other Gaudí works that are either closed off to the public or are outside Barcelona.

Upstairs is the famous **roof**, adorned with what look like giant medieval knights but are in fact the most photographed chimney pots in the world. Gaudí also wanted to erect a 12m statue of the Virgin up here and when Milà refused, he resigned from the project, vowing never to work for the bourgeoisie again. He then devoted the rest of his life to building La Sagrada Família.

INFORMATION

- ✉ Pg de Gràcia 92, L'Eixample
- ☎ 93 484 59 95
- Ⓜ Diagonal
- ◷ 10am-8pm
- ⑤ €6/3
- ⓘ guided tours Mon-Fri 6pm, Sat & Sun 11am; temporary exhibitions held; additional exhibitions in 2002 for International Gaudí Year
- ♿ good
- ✗ see p. 84-5

Martin Hughes

There's no smoke from these chimneys.

DON'T MISS
- the splendid panoramic views from the roof • the detail on the roof
- rooftop drinks and music on summer nights • the lift (ask one of the apartment attendants to show you)

LA RAMBLA (4)

Spain's most famous street is the main artery of old Barcelona and where visitors inevitably head upon arrival. Flanked by narrow traffic lanes, it is a broad, tree-lined pedestrian boulevard, crowded from dusk till dusk with the constant flow of locals and *giris* (out-of-towners). It may not be typical of Barcelona but it's the city's most extrovert side; a stage for an assortment of street performers, from flamenco dancers to fire-eaters and more human statues than you could possibly knock over in one go. It's dotted with overpriced pavement cafes and restaurants that nevertheless provide the perfect spot from which to take the city's pulse as you watch the flow of humanity saunter past. There's never a dull moment on La Rambla, whether your funny bone is being tickled, your enthusiasm for life being fuelled, or your pocket being picked.

INFORMATION

Ⓜ Catalunya, Liceu or Drassanes

✕ see p. 73

A flowering of artistic talent

La Rambla gets its name from a seasonal stream (*raml* in Arabic) that once ran here. It became a clogged sewer by the 14th century and was completely filled in by the 18th-century when trees were planted and mansions built along its sides. It is actually made up of five separate streets strung together, which is why you may hear it called Las Ramblas. At the top, Rambla de Canaletes is named after the century-old fountain that dispenses the purest water in the city. If you drink from it, locals say, you will some day return to Barcelona.

Postcards from the edge... of La Rambla.

DON'T MISS • the cocktail *del dia* at Boadas • a wander around La Boqueria market and a snack at Pinotxo • chocolates from Escribà • Mosaïc de Miró in Plaça de la Boqueria

MANZANA DE LA DISCORDIA   (5, H2)

This remarkable stretch of Pg de Gràcia is called the 'Block of Discord' because you'll find wildly contrasting works from the three greatest architects of Modernisme on it. In a classic case of keeping up with the Joneses, the esteemed architects were hired by the city's smartest families who clamoured to have their houses remodelled in the hip new style.

On the first corner, at No 35, is Domènech i Montaner's most lavish residence, **Casa Lleo Morera** (remodelled between 1902 and 1906). Its ground floor facade was ripped out in the 1940s by philistines and leather goods merchants, Loewe, who wanted bigger shop windows. But the decorative nymphs and reliefs – relating to the owner's work and hobbies – of the other floors remain intact. Try and sneak a peak inside to the spectacularly whimsical lobby.

Three doors up, at No 41, Puig i Cadafalch combined Gothic window frames, ceramic plaques and a stepped gable for the facade of the **Casa Amatller**, which, again, was inspired by the owner's life and pastimes. The pillared entrance hall and the staircase lit by stained glass are like the inside of some romantic castle. You can wander around the ground floor and pick up a Ruta del Modernisme ticket (see p. 35) before visiting the **Joierie Baguès**, which has a stunning collection of Modernista jewellery.

Casa Batlló, next door at No 43, is a Gaudí gem remodelled between 1905 and 1907. The facade is an allegory to St George and the dragon, its rippling skin sprinkled with bits of blue, mauve and green tile. If you stare long enough at the building, it seems almost to be a living being. You might fluke your way into the foyer if the main entrance is open.

⊠ 35-43 Pg de Gràcia,
L'Eixample
Ⓜ Passeig de Gràcia
✕ see p. 84-5

INFORMATION

Martin Hughes

Casa Batlló in all its quivering glory

A Dissenting Voice

At No 37 on this block is Enric Sagnier's neo-classical Casa Mulleras, remodelled in 1910. It is in itself discordant because it was a forerunner to Noucentisme (a reaction against the excesses of the unrestrained Modernisme).

LA SAGRADA FAMÍLIA (3, C6)

If you have time to see only one sight in Barcelona, this emblem of the city, and the work to which Gaudí dedicated most of his working life, should probably be it. It takes up a whole block of l'Eixample, has its own metro station and is the most talked about and visited unfinished building site in the world. After more than 120 years, the church is still only half complete.

INFORMATION

✉ Plaça de la Sagrada Família

☎ 93 207 30 31

🄴 www.sagradafamilia.org

Ⓜ Sagrada Família

🕐 Apr-Sept 9am-8pm, Oct-Mar 9am-6pm

💲 €5/3.70 (incl museum), €1.20 for lift up one of the towers, €3 for official guidebook

ⓘ information centre, guided tours (€3, 50mins) four times daily Mar-Oct, twice daily Fri-Mon Nov-Feb; special events

✕ kiosks near entrance

A Catholic group, the Josephines, commissioned the building of the Temple Expiatori de la Sagrada Família (Expiatory Temple of the Holy Family) in 1882. Ironically, the work with which Gaudí is most closely associated was neither begun, nor will be completed, by him. He replaced another architect in 1883, transformed the plans, and made it his sacred mission for the next 43 years until his death.

He planned three facades, dedicated to the Nativity, Passion and Glory (the main one, work on which hasn't even begun yet). Each is to be crowned by four towers, representing the 12 apostles. Four higher towers will symbolise the Evangelists while a colossal 173m-high central tower, flanked by a statue of the Virgin, will represent the Lord.

Only parts of the Nativity facade (facing C/de la Marina) were completed in Gaudí's time. He was meticulous about every detail and when asked why he fussed so much about the embellishments on the top of his towers – which nobody would ever see – he replied, 'the angels will see them'.

From 1912, he devoted all his energies exclusively to what had become his obsession. When funds – and enthusiasm – for the project dried up he helped by selling all his possessions and took to sleeping on site. No doubt mulling over some detail of its construction one day in 1926, a tram hit him.

One tip of La Sagrada, covered with gold

Such was his dishevelment by then that taxi drivers thought he was a tramp and at first refused to take him to hospital (where he later died).

In 1936, the year after Gaudí's assistants had completed the Nativity facade, anarchists broke into the workshops and destroyed all the plans and models they could find. The church seemed destined never to be built.

By 1954 the reinvigorated Josephines got the project rolling again and instructed architects basically to guess what Gaudí himself would have done. The pace of construction has accelerated in recent years, bankrolled principally by the 1.2 million people who visit the site each year.

Purists balk at the developments and say Gaudí's unfinished work should have been left intact as a monument to his genius. The plans have deviated from what 'God's architect' probably had in mind. In fact, the chief sculptor now is a committed atheist whose methods and work could hardly contrast more starkly with the originals. While Gaudí's Nativity facade is characteristically textured and detailed, the sculptures of Josep Maria Subirachs' Passion facade are bold and kitschy (and made with synthetic materials). The apse, which is more in line with Gaudí's thinking, should be completed and roofed in the next 10 years. Watch this space.

Whether you think the work-in-progress is a masterpiece or a monstrosity, you can't help but admire the dogged determination of Barcelona to get the job done. The Josephines, who commissioned the church 120 years ago, hope it will be finished by 2026, the centenary of Gaudí's death.

True perfectionism is for angels' eyes only.

DON'T MISS • the dream-like walk to the top of the towers • sketches in the museum of how the completed church will look • the perfect photograph (Nativity facade early morning, Passion late afternoon)

MUSEU D'HISTÒRIA DE LA CIUTAT (6, D5)

The entrance to this museum is through the 15th-century Gothic palace, Casa Padellàs, shifted here in 1931 to make way for the new road, Via Laietana. Digging the foundations one day, what should labourers stub their shovels on but the ancient Roman city of Barcino!

INFORMATION

- ✉ C/Veguer 2, Barri Gòtic
- ☎ 93 315 11 11
- Ⓜ Jaume I
- ◷ June-Sept: Tues-Sat 10am-8pm, Sun 10am-2pm; Oct-May: Tues-Sat 10am-2pm & 4pm-8pm, Sun 10am-2pm
- ⓢ €3/1.80
- ⓘ guided tours, exhibition video
- ✗ see p. 74-9

So, with a chance beginning, this remarkable and superbly presented museum – with the largest underground excavation of any ancient city in Europe – was born. You can take a spellbinding stroll through the town along glass ramps and peer down at the wheel ruts gouged into roads two millennia ago. Or explore public baths, drainage systems and a remarkably well preserved mosaic on the porch of a house. You can see storage areas used for wine and *garum* (a kind of fish sauce popular throughout the Roman empire) and, if you concentrate hard enough, they reckon you can still smell the pungent export. More than 4500 sq metres have been excavated so far, extending beneath Plaça del Rei and to the Catedral where you can see a Visigothic baptismal font.

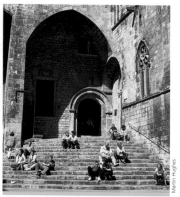

Discover what lies beneath...

After Barcino, you emerge into buildings of the former royal palace and can admire – among other treasures – the broad arches of the **Saló del Tinell**, a 14th-century banquet hall and an appropriate setting for King Fernando and Queen Isabel to nod and feign interest as Columbus breathlessly recounted something about discovering a 'New World'.

There's always lots to see here (even without the temporary exhibitions) and the museum considerately allows you to return again on the same ticket.

DON'T MISS • Capella Reial de Santa Àgata, the 14th-century palace chapel • the view from Mirador del Rei Martí • the invaluable information pamphlet in your language

MUSEU MARÍTIM (4, J5)

To appreciate what makes Barcelona unique, you must visit this museum, which provides a fascinating insight into the seafaring exploits upon which the city was built.

The Reials Drassanes (Royal Shipyards), completed in 1378, are a superb example of civic Catalan Gothic architecture. Up to 30 galleys could be built beneath their lofty arches at any one time and then slipped directly into the Mediterranean, which lapped the seaward side of the buildings until the 18th century. By then, there was no need to build ships here any more, and the yards were neglected until the 1980s when one of the city's most captivating exhibitions, the Museu Marítim, was installed.

The highlight is a life-size replica of Don Juan of Austria's flagship galley, which he successfully took into battle against the Turks off Lepanto in 1571, the last great sea struggle between fleets of galleys and a famous victory for Christianity. This battle, the history of maritime Barcelona and lots of kid-friendly adventures are presented in a series of simulations with headphone commentaries provided in English. Among the extensive collection of maritime paraphernalia are vessels of all types and epochs, from coastal fishing skips to giants of the steam age, as well as charts, paintings, instruments and figureheads. Outside the museum, alongside the Moll de la Fusta, you can board *Santa Eulàlia*, a 46m-long wooden sailing ship from 1918.

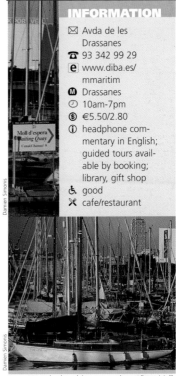

INFORMATION

- ✉ Avda de les Drassanes
- ☎ 93 342 99 29
- e www.diba.es/mmaritim
- Ⓜ Drassanes
- ⏲ 10am-7pm
- ⑤ €5.50/2.80
- ⓘ headphone commentary in English; guided tours available by booking; library, gift shop
- ♿ good
- ✗ cafe/restaurant

Watch the ships come in at Port Vell.

An ambitious expansion programme – which includes a plan to build a pond around the Drassanes – is under way and is due for completion in 2004.

DON'T MISS • the collection of *exuotos* (paintings made by sailors in gratitude to the saints) • plumbing the depths with one of the world's first submariners, Narcis Monturiol i Estarriol

MUSEU NACIONAL D'ART DE CATALUNYA (MNAC) (1, A2)

Fans of religious art will lose their minds with these extraordinary exhibitions of Romanesque and Gothic art, housed in the massive Palau Nacional, which was built as a *temporary* pavilion for the World Exhibition in 1929.

The unique Romanesque collection consists mainly of murals from 11th- and 12th-century churches in northern Catalunya, which art historians began salvaging in the 1920s. Figuring that you couldn't visit all of these deteriorating exhibitions on your own, at least not before private collectors gobbled them up, they were removed from crumbling walls and remounted here.

INFORMATION

✉ Palau Nacional, Parc de Montjuïc
☎ 93 622 03 60
e www.gencat.es/mnac
Ⓜ Espanya
🕐 Tues-Sat 10am-7pm, Sun 10am-2.30pm
$ €5
♿ excellent
✕ cafe-restaurant due to open late 2002

The result is a truly remarkable and mesmerising anthology of iconographic art. Even though some of them look like extras from *South Park,* the overall impression is strikingly bold with figures peering out hypnotically from reconstructed apses. Some columns bear the illustrative graffiti of monks, bored one afternoon, perhaps 1000 years ago. Frescoes, coins, carvings and elaborate altar frontals from the same churches complement the collection. One frontal (in section 5) depicts bewildered saints being boiled, having nails slammed into their heads and – always a crowd pleaser – being sawn in half from head to toe. 'Oh my God, they killed Kenny!'

The Gothic art is more decorative and plucked principally from churches in Barcelona itself. The collection makes for a fascinating study of the evolution of the genre and features international as well as Catalan works.

When the Museu d'Art Modern is relocated here some time in 2003, this will be an even brighter highlight with old and new Catalan art under the same roof.

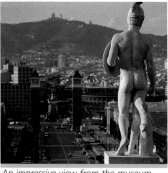

An impressive view from the museum

DON'T MISS
• the Gothic works of Catalans Bernat Martorell and Jaume Huguet
• *Crist de Taüll* (section 5) • the almost perfectly preserved mural from Sant Martí de Tost (section 4) • the outdoor escalators

MUSEU-MONESTIR DE PEDRALBES   (2, D2)

This uniquely peaceful corner of Barcelona provides an absorbing insight into medieval monastic life. It has become all the more fascinating since it acquired a chunk of the **Thyssen-Bornemisza Collection** (Col.lecció Thyssen-Bornemisza) of paintings from the 13th to 17th centuries (the rest of which are in Madrid).

The site features a convent that was founded in 1326, quickly built but scarcely touched since. It is considered a jewel of Catalan Gothic architecture and contains a lovely three-storey cloister, with a fountain and landscaped garden. It still functions as a convent, sheltering a small group of 'Poor Clares' who you can see shuffling behind grills erected to partition their closed quarters.

As you head around the cloister, you can inspect the trappings of convent life and visit the restored refectory, kitchen, stables, stores and infirmary, which houses a stunningly intricate series of dioramas on the life of Christ by Joan Mari. Built into the cloister walls are preserved day cells where the nuns spent most of their time in prayer and devotional reading.

The Thyssen-Bornemisza Collection is located in the spectacularly renovated nuns' dormitory. The 90 or so paintings are religious in theme and include works from European masters including Canaletto, Rubens, Tintoretto, Titian, Zurbarán and Velázquez. There are also works from the Renaissance period in Germany, some late baroque paintings and a collection of sculptures by anonymous medieval Italian artists.

INFORMATION

- ✉ Bda del Monestir 9, Pedralbes
- ☎ 93 280 14 34
- e www.museo thyssen.org
- 🚇 FGC to Reina Elisenda, then 10mins walk
- ⏰ Tues-Sun 10am-2pm
- 💲 €4.20/2.50
- ♿ good to Thyssen-Bornemisza Collection
- ✕ take a picnic to a nearby park (no food in the grounds)

Martin Hughes

Cloistered solitude for those 'Poor Clares'

DON'T MISS
- Fra Angelico's magnificent *Madonna of Humility* in the Thyssen-Bornemisza Collection • murals by Ferrer Bassá (1346) in the Capella de Sant Miquel

MUSEU PICASSO (4, E10)

Picasso spent many of his formative years in Barcelona, knocking about with the young upstarts who helped create Modernisme. He always had a soft spot for the city and in 1962 agreed to assist in the foundation of a museum here. His secretary and Barcelona buddy, Jaume Sabartés, donated his private collection, which was augmented by Picasso himself and then later by his widow.

INFORMATION

- ✉ C/de Montcada 15-23, La Ribera
- ☎ 93 319 63 10
- ⓔ www.museupicasso.bcn.es
- Ⓜ Jaume I
- ⊘ Tues-Sat 10am-8pm, Sun 10am-3pm
- Ⓢ €4.50/2.50
- ✗ see p. 81-3

Jonathan Chester

The museum is housed in a stunning row of 15th-century mansions. While it has some famous pieces, it is not a showcase for Picasso's most celebrated work. It focuses mainly on his early years and therefore provides a fascinating window into the formation of the 20th century's greatest artist.

The collection starts with the teenage Picasso's sketches, oils and doodlings, evidence of his precocious talent. It was only in the late 1890s that he began signing his works using his mother's last name and here the collection moves on to reveal Picasso's growing independence and individuality, at a time when he lived in a Barcelona studio away from his parents. The year 1900 was pivotal to his career: he had his first public exhibition in Els Quatre Gats cafe (p. 75), had his first taste of Paris and moved from sketching art scene buddies and street life into what's known as the Blue Period. The collection becomes more patchy after this, hopping through the Rose Period, skipping to the mature Cubism of 1917 and – just before you look up the Castilian for 'give me my money back' – it emerges into the extraordinary beauty of the Velázquez-inspired 1940s.

Finally, there is an extensive collection of his lithographs, ceramics and engravings.

Martin Hughes

Picasso changed the face of modern art.

DON'T MISS
- *Science and Charity* (1897), a realist work he painted for a competition, under parental pressure
- the menu for Els Quatre Gats, his first commission
- *Desamperados* (1904), typical of the Blue Period

PALAU DE LA MÚSICA CATALANA (4, B9)

Don't miss this concert hall, one of Barcelona's most brilliant highlights and celebrated by many as the crowning glory of Modernisme.

At the beginning of the 20th century, the Orfeo Català musical society asked Domènech i Montaner to build a temple to the Catalan Renaixença (Renaissance). The brief fired the enthusiasm of the fervent nationalist, and he gathered the best Catalan artisans of the age to help him with the task. Unpaid and cheesed off, Montaner didn't attend the opening in 1908 when his masterpiece was unveiled to universal acclaim.

Its bare-brick facade of mosaics, tile-clad pillars and busts only hints at the splendour within. By the use of glass, lampposts and the manipulation of natural light, Montaner blurs the distinction between inside and out. He considered the building 'the garden of music' and decoration blooms everywhere, among busts and sculptures that provide euphoric tributes to Catalan music and the music Catalans love.

But all this pales in comparison to the auditorium, a staggering symphony of ceramics and stained glass. Flanking the stage is a bust of Beethoven, a towering sculpture of Wagner's Valkyries, Josep Clavé and a medley of maidens. Muses, half ceramic and half sculpture, burst out from the back wall raring to join in on the performance. By day, light streams in from a spectacular stained-glass skylight, the centrepiece of the chamber. It is illuminated at night, providing distraction from the notoriously poor acoustics.

Damien Simons

Dale Buckton

Montaner's magical musical tour

INFORMATION

- ✉ C/Sant Françesc de Paula 2, La Ribera
- ☎ 93 295 72 00 or 93 268 10 00
- e www.palaumusica.org
- Ⓜ Urquinaona
- ⏱ 10am-3.30pm
- ⑤ €4.20/3.60
- ① guided tours (50mins) in English on the hour (tickets from Les Muses del Palau's shop at C/de Sant Pere més Alt 1); box office entrance around the side
- ♿ excellent
- ✕ see p. 81-3

DON'T MISS
- 'forest' balcony with 14 different pillar trees • a show, any show
- medieval-style chandeliers • the sympathetic restoration and extensions being carried out by Oscar Tusquets

PALAU GÜELL   (4, G5)

This mansion – one of the few Modernista buildings in the old quarters – is just a hop and a skip from La Rambla. It was Antoni Gaudí's first major work, built in the late 1880s for his patron, Eusebi Güell. Although somewhat muted by the flamboyant genius's standards, it is still a riot of different styles and materials (considered unworthy by the establishment of the time).

INFORMATION

- ✉ C/Nou de la Rambla 3-5, El Raval
- ☎ 93 317 39 74
- Ⓜ Liceu
- ⊘ Mon-Sat 10am-1pm & 4pm-7pm (prebooking advised)
- ⑤ €2.50/1.30
- ⓘ guided tours only (available in English)
- ✗ see p. 79-81

Martin Hughes

Martin Hughes

You'll rave about this roof.

The compulsory guided tour starts in the subterranean stables with fanning bare-brick pillars and arches, where police tortured political prisoners after the Civil War. Dark grey marble stairs lead to the first floor and a series of vestibules with columned galleries overhanging the street, designed to maximise space and natural light. The decoration becomes more ornate, and the original Modernista furniture more sumptuous, as you near the heart of the house, the salon. Functions and gatherings took place in this impressive room where the walls stretch up three floors to form a dome. What remains of the family chapel is reached through 5m panels made of hardwoods and ivory, and sheathed in horn and tortoiseshell. The family apartments on the next floor should have reopened by the time you read this.

The whole effect, while a masterfully crafted insight into Modernisme, is ostentatious and a little sombre. But all is forgiven when you emerge onto the rippled roof, a remarkable forest of unique chimney sculptures clad in colourful mosaics. From here you can peer over to a studio at No 6 where Picasso, who loathed Gaudí's work, began his Blue Period in 1902.

DON'T MISS
- the Modernisme furniture, which the tour passes over • the spy holes in the visitors' gallery (how Güell eavesdropped on guests) • the funnel used to drop coins to the poor outside

PARC GÜELL (3, A3)

The place where Gaudí turned his hand to landscape gardening is one of the most wonderful on the planet – a jovial and enchanting spot to relax, unwind and rub noses with the locals. It's not a sight to visit and tick off your list. It's a minor hassle to get here and can only be fully appreciated if you've got time in your pocket and relaxation on your mind.

The park originated in 1900 when Gaudí's patron, Eusebi Güell, commissioned him to create a garden suburb for the hoity-toity on a hill overlooking the city. The venture, a monumental commercial flop, was abandoned in 1914. But by then Gaudí, in his inimitable style, had created a unique space where the artificial almost seems more natural than the endeavours of Mother Nature.

Martin Hughes

INFORMATION

- ✉ C/d'Olot
- Ⓜ Lesseps (and a steep sign-posted walk) or Vallcarca
- 🚌 24 from Plaça Catalunya
- 🕐 June-Sept 9am-9pm; Apr, May & Oct 9am-8pm; Mar & Nov 9am-7pm; Dec-Feb 9am-6pm
- 💲 free
- 🍴 take a picnic

The lavishly ceramic-decorated entrance – guarded by a mosaic serpent, a favourite emblem of the city – is flanked by two fairytale-style houses. Another, off to your right, houses the Casa Museu Gaudí (p. 33). The steps lead to the **Sala Hipóstila**, a forest of 86 stone columns, originally intended to form a covered market. To the left a gallery with twisted stonework columns gives the impression of a cloister beneath tree roots – a motif repeated throughout the park. Above is a wonderful esplanade, the centrepiece of which is the **Banc de Trencadis**, a delightful bench that curves playfully around its perimeter and is clad with candy-coloured ceramics. Beyond here lies 3km of roads, walks and porticos that wind their way around the wooded hill, affording spectacular views of the city and ample opportunity to enjoy this mysterious place exactly how it was intended: as a park.

Gaudí's Assistant

The *trencadis* (fragmented tiles) you'll want to cosy up to on the bench of Parc Güell – as well as the ceramics that clad several other famous Gaudí buildings – are largely the work of Gaudí's associate, architect Josep Maria Jujol.

Martin Hughes

sights & activities

NEIGHBOURHOODS

To the east of **La Rambla**, Barcelona's main tourist artery, is the awesomely atmospheric **Barri Gòtic** (Gothic Quarter), the nucleus of the old city. Its medieval streets are lined with historic buildings and wonderful places to eat and drink. Across the noisy Via Laietena, is **La Ribera**, once the commercial centre of medieval Barcelona and home to some fascinating relics. Between it and the expansive **Parc Ciutadella** is the utterly hip district of **El Borne** (The Born), a magnet for style and a nub of exuberant nightlife. South of here is the revamped residential area of **Barceloneta**, most notable for its expansive waterside promenade. It's the gateway to the city's beaches, which lead up to (and beyond) **Port Olímpic**, a brash modern development with a huge marina and so-so restaurants and nightlife. **Port Vell** (Old Port), opposite the foot of La Rambla, has been transformed in recent years into a utilitarian leisure area.

On the other side of La Rambla is **El Raval**, once a hotbed of crime, poverty and sleaze but spruced up in recent years by the city fathers. While the northern half has been rejuvenated into an arty bohemian haven, what's left of Barri Xinès (Chinatown) is still not for the easily ruffled. Beyond this, the hill of **Montjuïc** is lined with parks, museums, Olympic installations and stunning city views.

The huge area of **L'Eixample** (The Extension) is Barcelona's economic core, a trove of Modernista treasures and home to the city's swankiest high couture. It connects the old quarters of Barcelona with **Gràcia**, a medieval village that was absorbed by the expanding city.

> ### Off the Beaten Track
>
> Only Barri Gòtic and La Rambla ever really feel swamped with tourists. But if you want to get away for some peace and quiet or just to hang out with the locals, you've got plenty of options. Peaceful parks and plaças abound (see pp. 38-40) while the neighbourhood of Gràcia (p. 18) gets very little tourist action, and a minor excursion from the city centre will bring you to the idyllic setting of Museu-Monestir de Pedralbes (p. 27).

Deep discussions on Barceloneta's pier as the sun goes down

Martin Hughes

MUSEUMS & ART GALLERIES

Casa Museu Gaudí
(3, A3) Worth a gander if you're in Parc Güell (p. 31), this is the house where Gaudí spent many of his later years. The museum includes some remarkable Modernista furniture, designed by Gaudí and his mates, along with some of his personal effects and a very narrow bed upon which he must have fantasised about completing La Sagrada Família.
✉ Parc Güell, Zona Alta ☎ 93 219 38 11 Ⓜ Lesseps, then a walk (follow the signs) ⊘ May-Sept 10am-8pm; Mar, Apr & Oct 10am-7pm; Nov-Feb 10am-6pm ⑤ €2.40

Centre de Cultura Contemporània de Barcelona (CCCB)
(4, B4) Loved by locals, this multi-use centre has a dynamic and cultured atmosphere. It occupies the shell of an 18th-century hospice and hosts a constantly changing programme of exhibitions on urban design, 20th-century arts, architecture and the city itself. It also organises and hosts dance performances, lectures and forums.
✉ C/de Montalegre 5, El Raval ☎ 93 306 41 00 Ⓔ www.cccb.org Ⓜ Universitat ⊘ Tues, Thur & Fri 11am-2pm & 4-8pm, Wed & Sat 11am-8pm, Sun 10am-3pm ⑤ varies ♿ excellent

Fundació Antoni Tàpies (5, H2)
This Domènech i Montaner building – considered by many to be the prototype for Modernisme – houses the experimental work of Catalan's greatest living artist, Antoni Tàpies, as well as exhibitions by other contemporary artists. The building is crowned with coiled wire, a Tàpies sculpture titled *Núvol in Cadira* (Cloud and Chair), which looks interesting by day and spectacular by night.
✉ C/d'Aragò 255, L'Eixample ☎ 93 487 03 15 Ⓜ Passeig de Gràcia ⊘ Tues-Sun 10am-8pm ⑤ €4.20/2.10 ♿ excellent

Fundación Francisco Godia (5, H2)
A private collection featuring an intriguing mix of medieval art, ceramics and modern paintings. It's next door to the **Museu Egipci** (p. 35); a joint ticket to both is available.
✉ C/de Valencia 284 pral, L'Eixample ☎ 93 272 31 80 Ⓔ www.fundacionfgodia.org Ⓜ Passeig de Gràcia ⊘ Wed-Mon 10am-8pm ⑤ €4.20

Galeria Maeght
(4, E10) After the crowds of the Museu Picasso, it's a calming and sensual treat to walk around this gallery, which occupies a beautiful 16th-century mansion nearby. It's the local branch of the famous Paris-based outfit, and showcases the works of established painters and sculptors from Spain and Europe.
✉ C/de Montcada 25, La Ribera ☎ 93 310 42 45 Ⓜ Jaume I ⊘ Tues-Sat 10am-2pm & 4-8pm ⑤ free ♿ fair

Galeria Olímpica
(1, C3) A museum chock-full of photographs and memorabilia associated with the 1992 Barcelona Olympics – one for dedicated anoraks.
✉ Estadi Olímpic, Pg Olímpic, Montjuïc ☎ 93 426 06 60 Ⓜ Paral.lel, then Funicular de Montjuïc ⊘ Apr-Sep Tues-Sat 10am-2pm & 4-8pm, Sun 10am-2pm; Oct-Mar Tues-Sat 10am-1pm & 4-6pm, Sun 10am-2pm ⑤ €2.40 ♿ good

Museu Barbier-Mueller d'Art Precolombí (4, E10)
A branch of the prestigious Barbier-Mueller museum in Geneva, here you'll find a wonderful assortment of art from the pre-Columbian civilisations of Central and South America. The rotating exhibition is over dramatically presented but stunning nevertheless.
✉ C/de Montcada 14, La Ribera ☎ 93 319 76 03 Ⓜ Jaume I ⊘ Tues-Sat 10am-8pm, Sun 10am-3pm ⑤ €3/1.50 (combined ticket with Museu Tèxtil i d'Indumentària p. 37)

Museu d'Arqueologia (1, A4)
This well presented archaeology museum mainly features artefacts discovered in Catalunya and Mediterranean Spain, ranging from copies of pre-Neanderthal skulls to jewel-studded Visigoth crosses. With ongoing discoveries it's getting even better all the time. It also

features a statue of a splendidly endowed, and routinely aroused, Priapus (the God of male procreative power) that we're not allowed to inspect closely.
✉ **Pg de Santa Madrona 39-41, Montjuïc** ☎ **93 423 21 49** e www.mac.es ⓜ **Poble Sec** ⊙ **Tues & Thur 10am-7pm, Wed & Fri-Sun 10am-3pm** ⑤ €2.40/1.80 ♿ **excellent**

Museu d'Art Contemporani de Barcelona (MACBA)
(4, B4) This gleaming glassy structure was dropped on El Raval in 1995 and, after a few years finding its way, now shines out as a stage for the best of Catalan, Spanish and international contemporary art. Its permanent collection broadly starts where the Museu Nacional d'Art Modern de Catalunya (p. 36-7) stops.
✉ **Plaça dels Àngels 1, El Raval** ☎ **93 412 08 10** e www.macba.es ⓜ **Universitat** ⊙ **Mon & Wed-Fri 11am-7.30pm, Sat 10am-8pm, Sun 10am-3pm** ⑤ €4.80/3.30, all €2.40 on Wed ♿ **excellent**

Museu de Ceràmica
(2, F3) This attractive museum has perhaps the most fragile exhibits in Barcelona: an exceptional collection of Spanish ceramics from medieval times to the present day. It includes some pieces by Miró and Picasso, as well as a charming section of tiles depicting Catalan life.
✉ **Palau Reial de Pedralbes, Avda Diagonal 686, Zona**

Museu d'Art Contemporani de Barcelona (MACBA)

Alta ☎ **93 280 16 21** ⓜ **Palau Reial** ⊙ **Tues-Sat 10am-6pm (until 3pm Sun & hols)** ⑤ €2.40 (€4.30 joint with Museu de les Arts Decoratives)

Museu de Geologia
(4, D12) If geology doesn't grab you, neither will this vast collection of minerals, rocks and fossils in the city's oldest municipal museum.
✉ **Parc de la Ciutadella** ☎ **93 319 68 95** e www.museu geologia.bcn.es ⓜ **Arc de Triomf** ⊙ **Tues-Sun 10am-2pm (until 6.30pm Thur)** ⑤ €2.40/1.80

Museu de la Música
(5, F2) An international ensemble of musical instruments dating from the 16th century, set in a Modernista gem by Puig i Cadafalch. The highlight is a collection of guitars tracing the evolution of the instrument from its Andalucían origins more than 200 years ago.
✉ **Avda Diagonal 373,**

L'Eixample ☎ **93 416 11 57** ⓜ **Diagonal** ⊙ **Tues-Sun 10am-2pm (until 8pm Wed in summer)** ⑤ €2.50

Museu de les Arts Decoratives
(2, F3) Occupying the same former palace as the Museu de Ceràmica, this series of galleries overlooks a stunningly sumptuous oval throne room and features a constantly rotating collection of furniture and decorative objects from the early Middle Ages onwards.
✉ **Palau Reial de Pedralbes, Avda Diagonal 686, Zona Alta** ☎ **93 280 50 24** e www.bcn.es/icub ⓜ **Palau Reial** ⊙ **Tues-Sat 10am-6pm (until 3pm Sun & hols)** ⑤ €2.40 (€4.30 joint with Museu de Ceràmica) ♿ **excellent**

Museu de Zoologia
(4, D12) This rather fusty old institution is the place for stuffed animals, model

elephants and skeletons of huge things that lived in the past.
✉ **Parc de la Ciutadella, La Ribera** ☎ 93 319 69 12 Ⓜ Arc de Triomf ☺ Tues-Sun 10am-2pm (until 6.30pm Thur) Ⓢ €2.50 ♿ excellent

Museu del Parfum

(5, J2) A thoroughly unexpected treat, this museum (at the back of a shop) features hundreds of perfume receptacles and bottles, ranging from pre-dynastic Egypt to modern times, which you can look at but unfortunately not sniff. More, it's like a glass microcosm of the evolution of design.
✉ **Perfumeria Regia, Pg de Gràcia 39, L'Eixample** ☎ 93 215 72 38 Ⓔ www.perfum -museum.com Ⓜ Passeig de Gràcia ☺ Mon-Fri 10am-8.30pm, Sat 10.30am-2pm & 5-8.30pm Ⓢ free ♿ good

Museu d'Història de Catalunya (4, H11)

Inside the modernised warehouses of the Palau de Mar building, this museum is a hectic interactive exploration of 2000 years of Catalan history, from the Romans to the current day. An English guidebook is available from reception. Don't miss the view from the top floor restaurant.
✉ **Plaça de Pau Vila, Barceloneta** ☎ 93 225 47 00 Ⓔ www.cultura .gencat.es/museus/mhc/ Ⓜ Barceloneta ☺ Tues-Thur 10am-7pm, Fri & Sat 10am-8pm, Sun 10am-2.30pm Ⓢ €3/2.10 ♿ excellent

Barcelona Discounts

As well as checking out flyers in bars and cafes for cheap deals, you can take advantage of one of the following cards.

Articket costs €15 and allows you entry to six of the city's main art spaces: Museu Nacional d'Art de Catalunya (MNAC), the Fundació Joan Miró and Antonio Tàpies, the Centre de Cultura Contemporània de Barcelona (CCCB), and the Museu d'Art Contemporani de Barcelona (MACBA).

The **Barcelona Card** is very handy if you intend blitzing through the sights. Valid for between one and three days, it gives you unlimited transport on the metro and buses, a discount on Aerobús, discounts of up to 50% at a wide range of attractions as well as minor discounts on some shops and restaurants. A list of participating places comes with the card; it costs €15.70/12.70 for one day, €18.70/15.60 for two days and €21.70/18.70 for three days.

Both the Articket and Barcelona Card are available from the tourist office at Plaça Catalunya 17 (4, A7; ☎ 906 30 12 52; 9am-9pm) and all other tourist offices.

And Modernista enthusiasts should check out **Ruta del Modernisme**, a multi-access ticket that lasts for 30 days and entitles you to half-price admission into most of the major works by Gaudí and his mates. It's available from Casa Amatller (5, H2; Pg de Gràcia, L'Eixample; ☎ 93 488 01 39; 10am-7pm) and costs €3.60/2.50.

Martin Hughes

Museu Egipci (5, H2)

An incredible private collection featuring more than 500 exhibits including ceramics, mummies, friezes, jewellery, masks and statuettes from ancient Egypt. A joint ticket with neighbour **Fundación Francisco** Godia (p. 33) is available.
✉ **C/de Valencia 284, L'Eixample** ☎ 93 488 01 88 Ⓔ www.fund clos.com Ⓜ Passeig de Gràcia ☺ Mon-Sat 10am-2pm & 4-8pm, Sun 10am-2pm Ⓢ €5.50 ♿ good

Rolling with the Crowds

You can't fully appreciate the subtlety of Miró or the genius of Gaudí when you're standing on your tippy-toes looking over somebody else's shoulder. Unfortunately, there's no sure way of beating the crowds and queues form at the most popular sights before the box office even opens. La Sagrada Família is at its best in the early evening when the coach tours retire to their buffets, the Museu Picasso settles down around lunchtime and Joan Miró looks his best in the morning. The crowds generally surge and recede at the busiest places so if the numbers are getting you down just retire to the nearest cafe and wait. When the cafe fills up, it's a good time to see the sight.

Museu Etnològic

(1, A3) Only tiny chunks of this enormous collection of ethnological exhibits from non-European cultures are shown at any one time. The museum tries to present them in context rather than just as exotic objects but if you're dithering about going, you're not interested enough.

✉ **Pg de Santa Madrona, Montjuïc**
☎ 93 424 68 07
Ⓜ **Poble Sec** ◷ **Tues & Thur 10am-7pm, Wed & Fri-Sun 10am-3pm**
Ⓢ €2.40

Museu Frederic Marès (6, B4)

A mind-boggling, multi-brow and fascinating collection of everyday items, art and sculpture amassed by Frederic Marès i Deulovol (1893-1991), a rich sculptor, traveller and hoarder extraordinaire. Considering its scope, the collection is presented remarkably cohesively although you may still need to catch your breath in the delightful courtyard cafe.

✉ **Plaça Sant Iu 5-6, Barri Gòtic**

☎ 93 310 58 00
Ⓜ **Jaume I** ◷ **Tues & Thur 10am-5pm, Wed, Fri & Sat 10am-7pm, Sun 10am-3pm**
Ⓢ €3/1.80

Museu Militar (1, C5)

An assortment of weapons, uniforms, armour, tin soldiers and instruments of war from around the world make up this sombre collection, housed in an 18th-century fortress overlooking Barcelona (which was used more for bombarding the city than defending it). The view is magnificent.

✉ **Castell de Montjuïc, Montjuïc** ☎ 93 329 86 13 Ⓜ **Paral.lel**, then **Funicular de Montjuïc**, then **Telèferic de Montjuïc** ◷ (unreliable) **June-Sept Tues-Sun 9.30am-8pm; Oct-May Tues-Sat 9.30am-7pm** Ⓢ €1.50

Museu Nacional d'Art Modern de Catalunya (4, F14)

Not quite 'modern' art as you might expect, this

Museu Nacional d'Art Modern de Catalunya

gallery exhibits Catalan works from the 1850s to 1930s. It is most interesting, therefore, as a showcase of the artistic explosion associated with the Modernism era and as such is well worth a visit. Note that plans are afoot to move this collection to a mega museum in Montjuïc's Palau Nacional by 2003.

✉ **Edifici del Parlament, Parc de la**

Ciutadella, La Ribera
☎ 93 319 57 28
🅔 www.mnac.es
Ⓜ Ciutadella
🕐 Tues-Sat 10am-7pm, Sun 10am-2.30pm
💲 €3

Museu Tèxtil i d'Indumentària (4, E10)
This dimly lit (and non-airconditioned) textile and costume museum occupies a 13th-century mansion.

A visit here is a must for anyone interested in the evolution of fashion and fabrics and features garments from baroque to Pravda.

✉ **C/de Montcada 12, La Ribera** ☎ 93 319 76 03 Ⓜ Jaume I 🕐 Tues-Sat 10am-6pm, Sun 10am-3pm 💲 €3/1.50 **(combined ticket with Museu Barbier-Mueller d'Art Precolombí p. 33)**

CHURCHES & CATHEDRALS

Capella d'En Marcús (4, D10)
This oft unnoticed, and neglected, little Romanesque chapel was built in the 12th century to provide shelter and alms to travellers who arrived after the city gates had closed for the night. It is only open for worship and has no regular schedule.

✉ **Placeta Marcús, La Ribera** Ⓜ Jaume I

Església de Sant Pau del Camp (4, G2)
Barcelona's oldest church provides a peaceful haven in the occasionally repellent El Raval. Monks founded 'St Paul in the Fields' in the 9th century when it was located a world away from the city. The squat little rural-looking church looks its age but has some wonderful Visigothic decoration on its doorway.

✉ **C/de Sant Pau 101, El Raval** Ⓜ Paral.lel 🕐 Wed-Mon 11.30am-1pm & 6-7.30pm, Tues 11.30am-12.30pm

Església de Sant Pere de les Puelles (4, B11)
Although altered beyond recognition since it was first established by the Visigoths,

this fortress-like church has a remarkable history. When the Moors invaded in the 10th century the *puelles* (an order of young nuns renowned for their beauty) cut off their own noses to protect themselves from attack. Marginally miffed, the invaders chopped their heads off as well.

✉ **Plaça de Sant Pere, La Ribera** Ⓜ Arc de Triomf 🕐 8.30-9.30am & 7-8.30pm

Església de Santa Anna (4, B7)
Occupying a tranquil little square, this simple and

unassuming Romanesque chapel (founded in the 12th century) has a peaceful cloister enclosing a garden and fountain.

✉ **C/de Santa Anna, Barri Gòtic**
Ⓜ Catalunya
🕐 **(unreliable) 9am-1pm & 6.30-8.30pm**

Església de Santa Maria del Mar (4, F10)
This Catalan Gothic church, built between 1329 and 1384, is Barcelona's finest. It looks unexceptional from the outside but the immensity of the scale and purity of its proportions within

Setmana Tràgica

The conscription of young Catalans for Spain's imperialist war in Morocco lit the fuse of anarchism among disaffected workers in Barcelona in 1909. Protests and strikes spilled over into full-scale rioting against the establishment and some 70 churches were torched during what came to be known as Setmana Tràgica (Tragic Week). Thanks to the presence of an armed guard, the Catedral was one of only a handful of churches spared. The anarchists attracted much popular support, particularly after the army executed many of its leaders (including the more moderate) and Barcelona became known as 'anarchism's rose of fire'.

will take your breath away. Anarchists gutted it in 1936, thus clearing it of decoration and allowing its extraordinary features to stand out even more.

✉ Plaça de Santa Maria del Mar, La Ribera Ⓜ Jaume I
🕐 9am-1.30pm & 4.30-8pm

Església de Santa Maria del Pi (4, E6)

This striking church, built between 1322 and 1453, is considered a classic example of Catalan Gothic architecture with an imposing facade, a wide interior, no aisles and a single nave. The beautiful rose window above its entrance is thought to be the world's largest.

✉ Plaça del Pi, Barri Gòtic Ⓜ Liceu
🕐 8.30am-1pm & 4.30-9pm

Barcelona's Gothic Catedral (p. 16)

Temple del Sagrat Cor (2, A3)

Crowning Tibidabo, and seen from many parts of the city, this church was built by way of atonement for the Setmana Tràgica (p. 37) of 1909 and modelled on the Sacré Coeur in Paris. It is even more vilified by aesthetes but has a lift to the roof with staggering views.

✉ Plaça del Tibidabo
🚋 FGC Tibidabo, then Tramvia Blau 🕐 8am-7pm ⑤ €0.60 for lift

PLAÇAS, PARKS & SPACES

Antic Hospital de la Santa Creu (4, D4)

Gaudí died at this 15th-century hospital, which now houses Catalunya's national library and an arts school. It has a delightful, if somewhat dilapidated, colonnaded courtyard where you can hang out listening to music students practising on the steps while resisting the charms of pongy tramps offering booze and wisdom.

✉ C/del Carme 47, El Raval Ⓜ Liceu
🕐 Mon-Fri 9am-8pm, Sat 9am-2pm

La Rambla del Raval (4, F3)

As part of the city's plan to clean up El Raval, this broad pedestrian area was created in 2000 as a breath of fresh air for the congested neighbourhood.

✉ El Raval
Ⓜ Liceu or Paral.lel

Parc de la Ciutadella (4, F13)

Formerly the site of a fort used by Madrid to suppress Catalan nationalism, this is now a wonderful space to chill and expand. A young Gaudí assisted the park's architect Josep Fontsère in building the impressive *cascada* (waterfalls). There's plenty of boating and bongo drums in summer and the park is also home to the zoo and several museums.

✉ Pg de Picasso, La Ribera Ⓜ Arc de Triomf

🕐 10am until approx ½hr before sunset

Parc d'Espanya Industrial (3, H1)

Maligned by many, this playfully post-modern park comprises what look like galactic watchtowers overlooking a boating lake and

No poodles in Parc de la Ciutadella!

a dragon sculpture that's popular with kiddies. It is transformed when illuminated at night and worth a look if you're waiting for a train at Estació Sants.

✉ Pg de Antoni, Sants
Ⓜ Sants Estació
🕒 10am until approx ½hr before sunset

Parc Joan Miró (3, H2)

Miró's giant phallic sculpture *Dona i Ocell* (Woman and Bird) is the only attraction in this large dirt space, known by locals as Parc de l'Escorxador (Abbatoir Park) because it used to be a slaughterhouse for the now defunct bullring across the road. Renovations were underway at time of research so it might be spruced up.

✉ C/de Tarragona, L'Eixample
Ⓜ Tarragona 🕒 10am until approx ½hr before sunset

Pg Marítim de la Barceloneta (3, G10)

This 1.25km promenade along the beach from La Barceloneta to Port Olímpic, through an area that used to look like a railway junkyard, makes for a very pleasant stroll, jog or blade.

✉ Barceloneta
Ⓜ Ciutadella Vila Olímpic

Plaça de Catalunya

(4, A6) Surrounded by banks and department stores, this huge square connects the cities old and new and is the hub of Barcelona's human and pigeon life. Post-siesta it's often standing room only among the sculptures and fountains.

✉ L'Eixample
Ⓜ Catalunya

Plaça de George Orwell (4, F7)

Dubbed 'Plaça del Trippy' by the effervescent student crowd that socialises here, this newish triangular space seems to be in a custody battle between tourists, students, new age hippies and the homeless contingent.

✉ Barri Gòtic Ⓜ Liceu

Plaça de la Vila de Madrid (4, C6)

Sorely neglected over the years, this square with excavated Roman tombs seems to be in a tourist blind spot. There was renovation work going on at the time of writing and the result should be worth a look.

✉ Barri Gòtic
Ⓜ Catalunya

Plaça de Sant Jaume (6, E3)

El lugar donde se cocina todo (the place where everything gets cooked), this square has been the centre of Barcelona's civic life since the Romans first hung their helmets here.

✉ Barri Gòtic
Ⓜ Jaume I

Plaça de Sant Josep Oriol & Plaça del Pi

(4, E6) These atmospheric conjoined squares nestle

beneath the towering Església de Santa Maria del Pi. They are both lined with cafes, buskers and cheerful souls, and reached by numerous quaint narrow streets.

✉ Barri Gòtic Ⓜ Liceu

Plaça de Sant Just (4, E8)

A captivating medieval square with a peculiarly positive vibe and a water fountain dating from 1367. This is also the site where, during a political demonstration, Gaudí spoke Catalan to a policeman and ended up spending a night in the slammer.

✉ Barri Gòtic
Ⓜ Jaume I

Plaça de Santa Maria del Mar (4, F10)

This is one of the city's prettiest spaces and offers the perfect vantage point from which to view the stunning church of the same name while enjoying some delightful terrace dining and sipping.

✉ La Ribera Ⓜ Jaume I

Plaça del Rei (6, C5)

In this wholly preserved medieval courtyard, King Fernando reputedly greeted

Relaxing in the sun in the Barri Gòtic

A Fine Eixample

Ildefons Cerdà is the man responsible for the revolutionary design of the grid-like Eixample (Extension) into which Barcelona grew in the 19th century. However, developers disregarded the more utopian features of his design, which called for building on only two sides of each block and the provision of gardens within. Now, nearly 150 years later, the city is trying to reclaim these public spaces. The garden around the Torre de les Aigues water tower (5, J4) at C/de Roger de Llúria 56 offers a peek at how perfect Cerdà's plan could have been.

Christopher Columbus upon his return from discovering the new world. It is surrounded by buildings of the Palau Reial, most of which are now open to visitors as the Museu d'Història de la Ciutat (p. 24).
⊠ **Barri Gòtic**
Ⓜ **Jaume I**

Plaça del Sol (3, C4)
This gregarious square – where the young folk of Gràcia converge on weekend evenings – is lined with bars and eateries, and is a great place to come when alfresco is paramount.
⊠ **Gràcia** Ⓜ **Fontana**

Plaça dels Àngels
(4, C4) Conceived as a parade ground for an artsy crowd, this wide space in front of MACBA (p. 34) has been overrun by gleeful skaters and trick-bikers who seem to have more spills than thrills on the low wall.
⊠ **El Raval**
Ⓜ **Universitat**

Plaça Reial (4, F6)
A pretty, expansive square with neo-classical facades, palm trees and numerous restaurants and bars. Once notorious for poverty and crime, it still has a jaunty

edginess and locals say if you get your wallet stolen on Tuesday, you can come here on Wednesday to buy it back. The elegant lampposts were Gaudí's first commission.
⊠ **Barri Gòtic**
Ⓜ **Liceu**

Plaça Rius i Taulet
(5, D2) An atmospheric square dominated by a 125ft clock tower, which is adorned with signs of the zodiac. This is the soul of Gràcia and site of its 19th-century town hall.
⊠ **Gràcia**
Ⓜ **Diagonal or Fontana**

Plaça Sant Felip Neri (6, C2)
This ambient place, around a soothing fountain, is in the shadow of the church of the same name (where Gaudí worshipped daily and was heading the day the tram caught him). The damage to the church walls is testament to its former function as an execution yard during the Civil War, a silent monument to the martyrs who died here.
⊠ **Barri Gòtic** Ⓜ **Liceu**

PUBLIC ART

Barcelona's wealth of public artworks is the result of an innovative project started by the city council in the 1970s to revitalise individual neighbourhoods. With the offer of a blank canvas and all expenses paid artists from around the world worked for a fraction of their market rates and created these engaging pieces of art to decorate the city.

Barcelona Head (4, H9)
Designed by the American pop artist Roy Lichtenstein in 1992, this 14m sculpture on the border of La Ribera and the shoreline is impossible to miss. The broken ceramic coating is believed to be a homage to

Gaudí.
⊠ **Barceloneta**
Ⓜ **Barceloneta**

David-Goliat (3, F10)
Beneath the two skyscrapers of the Olympic village, Antoni Llena's wonderful sculpture from

1993 honours the poor who were uprooted from this neighbourhood. It consists of a large metal sheet shaped like a mask and suspended 20m up on three steel tubes, depicting Goliath exposed to the

elements.
✉ **Port Olímpic**
Ⓜ **Ciutadella Vila Olímpica**

Dona i Ocell (3, H2)
One of the symbols of Barcelona, *Woman and Bird* was Joan Miró's last large sculpture, inaugurated in 1981, the year of his death. It was made in collaboration with the ceramist Joan Gardy Artigas.
✉ **Sants** Ⓜ **Tarragona**

Gat (4, H5)
Popular with the locals, this giant and tubby tabby is the work of Columbian artist Fernando Botero and was unveiled in 1992.
✉ **El Raval**
Ⓜ **Drassanes**

Homenatge a l'Exposiciò Universal del 1888 (4, C13)
Loathed by many locals – and included here just out of devilment – this homage to urban transformation, by Antoni Clavè (1991), can be found in Barcelona's oldest park, the site of the 1888 Universal Exhibition.
✉ **Parc de la Ciutadella**
Ⓜ **Barceloneta** or **Arc de Triomf**

Homenatge a Picasso
(4, E12) This compelling piece by Antoni Tàpies was commissioned by the city council in 1983 on the centennial anniversary of Picasso's birth. Old furniture, sheets and steel girders are assembled inside a large glass box and distorted by a film of water running down the panels. Beware the buses that speed down this slip road.
✉ **Pg Picasso, La Ribera** Ⓜ **Barceloneta**

L'Estel Ferit (3, J9)
American Rebecca Horn's striking tribute to Barceloneta stands on the beach and is a column of rusted iron and glass cubes, illuminated at night.
✉ **Barceloneta**
Ⓜ **Barceloneta**

Mosaic de Miró (4, E6)
Smack bang in the middle of La Rambla, look out for this colourful mosaic painted by Joan Miró in 1976, when he also signed one of the bricks.
✉ **La Rambla** Ⓜ **Liceu**

Peix (3, F10)
American Frank Gehry's smooth and glistening copper *Fish* sculpture was installed for the Olympics and can be admired all along the beaches and promenades.
✉ **Port Olympic**
Ⓜ **Ciutadella Vila Olímpica**

David & Goliat

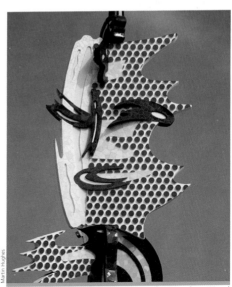

Not just a pretty face... the Barcelona Head

NOTABLE BUILDINGS & MONUMENTS

Ajuntament (6, E3)

Also known as the Casa de la Ciutat, this town hall has been the seat of city power since the 14th century and has a Catalan Gothic side facade on C/de la Ciutat. Belying its blandly renovated neo-classical front is a spectacular interior featuring golden mural holograms, a majestic staircase and the splendidly restored chamber Saló de Cent.

✉ Plaça de Sant Jaume, Barri Gòtic ☎ 93 402 73 64 ℮ www.bcn.es Ⓜ Jaume I ◷ Sat & Sun 10am-2pm Ⓢ free ♿ good

Arc de Triomf (4, B12)

This curious Josep Vilaseca monument, with its Islamic-style brickwork, was the ceremonial entrance to the 1888 Unviersal Exhibition, Barcelona's first spirited

Arc de Triomf

attempt to put itself on the world map. Exactly what triumph it commemorates isn't clear – probably just getting the thing built in time for the exhibition.

✉ Pg Lluís Companys, La Ribera Ⓜ Arc de Triomf

Casa Calvet (5, K4)

Gaudí's first apartment block, and most conventional building, is interesting because it won him the only award of his life, the city council's prize for the best building of 1900. Sober and straight from the outside, some hints of whimsy can be seen in the ground floor restaurant (see p. 84).

✉ C/de Casp 48, L'Eixample ☎ 93 412 40 12 Ⓜ Urquinaona Ⓢ €3 ♿ good

Casa de l'Ardiaca

(6, B3) This 14th-century house is home to the city's archives and has a supremely serene courtyard, renovated by Domènech i Montaner in 1902 when the building was owned by the lawyers' college. He also designed the postal slot, which is adorned with swallows and a tortoise, said to represent

the swiftness of truth and the plodding pace of justice.

✉ C/de Santa Llúcia 1, Barri Gòtic Ⓜ Jaume I ◷ Mon-Sat 10am-2pm & 4-8pm

Casa de les Punxes

(5, F3) Puig i Cadafalch could have been eating too much cheese late at night when he created this neo-Gothic fantasy, which was built between 1903 and 1905. Officially the Casa Terrades, its pointed turrets earned it the popular nickname Casa de les Punxes (House of the Spikes).

✉ Avda Diagona 420, L'Eixample Ⓜ Diagonal

Castell dels Tres Dragons (4, D12)

The only Domènech i Montaner structure built for the Universal Exhibition of 1888 and not demolished immediately afterwards, this building was a forerunner to Modernisme with its innovative use of exposed plain brick and iron, capped by ceramic decoration. It now houses the Museu de Zoologia.

✉ Parc de la Ciutadella, La Ribera Ⓜ Arc de Triomf

Touched by the Mushroom

Señor Calvet, the man who commisioned a young Gaudí to build Casa Calvet, was a connoisseur of mushrooms and is believed to have stimulated Gaudí's interest in all things funghi. Later in the architect's flamboyant career, particularly after Parc Güell, rumour raced around town that he was, in fact, 'touched by the mushroom'. Hallucinogenics aside, after Casa Calvet, Gaudí rarely drew another straight line.

Editorial Montaner i Simòn (Fundació Antoni Tàpies) (5, H2)

Considered to be a prototype for Modernisme, this Domènech i Montaner building was the first in the city with an iron frame and displays the architect's penchant for bare brick and iron. Originally built for his brother, the renovations were carried out by his grandson when the building was transformed into the Fundació (p. 33).

✉ C/d'Aragò 255, L'Eixample Ⓜ Passeig de Gràcia

L'Anella Olímpic & Estadi Olímpic (1, B3)

For sports fans, L'Anella Olímpica (Olympic Ring) is the group of installations built for the main events of the 1992 Olympics. They include the Estadi Olímpic, which is open to the public when Espanyol (the 'other' football team) isn't getting whipped.

✉ Pg Olímpic, Montjuïc ☎ 93 426 20 89 Ⓜ Paral.lel, then Funicular de Montjuïc ⏱ 10am-6pm (until 8pm in summer) ⑨ free

Farmàcia Nordbeck (5, K5)

For whatever reason, pharmacies and Modernisme had a very tight relationship in l'Eixample. With its stained glass, dark wood and sinuous design, this 1905 building is a prime example of how asking a stranger for haemorrhoid cream needn't be such a trauma.

✉ C/d'Ausia Marc 31, L'Eixample Ⓜ Urquinaona

Gran Teatre del Liceu (4, F5)

A welder's stray spark caused a fire that gutted Barcelona's famous 19th-century opera house in 1994. Recreated, remodelled and reopened in late 1999, this lustrous and luxurious new theatre can be visited by guided tour (or you can see the visual presentation on TV at the corner of C/de Sant Pau and La Rambla).

✉ La Rambla 51-59 ☎ 93 485 99 00 Ⓔ www.liceu barcelona.com Ⓜ Liceu ⏱ tours 9.45-11am (booking necessary) ⑨ €5 for tours ♿ excellent

Hospital de la Santa Creu i de Sant Pau (3, A6)

A Domènech i Montaner masterpiece, begun in 1901 and finished by his son in 1930. This uniquely chirpy hospital is a gargantuan Modernista landmark comprising 48 unique and lavishly decorated pavilions, separated by gardens and connected by underground tunnels. Feign illness or just wander around the gardens.

✉ C/de Sant Antoni Mara Claret 167, La Sagrada Família Ⓜ Hospital de Sant Pau

Llotja (4, G10)

This 14th-century building housed the old stock exchange and was once an arts school attended by Picasso and Miró. The exterior is 18th-century neo-classical but the original Gothic hall is said to be superb. Unfortunately, it is off-limits to tourists.

✉ C/del Consolat de Mar 2, La Ribera Ⓜ Barceloneta or Jaume I

Mercat del Born (4, E11)

Looming over Pg del Borne, this extraordinary feat of engineering is an 1870s wrought-iron 'shed' with a roof swathed in patterned tiles. From the light-filled interior the roof appears to hover above the space. Once the city's main wholesale market, which relocated in 1971, the structure is being renovated to house a library and arts centre.

✉ Plaça Comercial, La Ribera Ⓜ Jaume I

Monument a Colom (4, J6)

Columbus gave the first report of his discoveries in the Americas to the delighted Catholic Monarchs in Barcelona and many, many years later this 50m monument to him was built for the Universal Exhibition in 1888. Sometimes it feels like he's urging the tourist throngs to go elsewhere but you can catch a lift to the soles of his feet for a fine view.

✉ La Rambla ☎ 93 302 52 24 Ⓜ Drassanes

Roman Walls

Of course, the city's first architects of note were the Romans who built a town here in the first century BC. Large relics of the 3rd and 4th century walls that marked the boundary of this town can still be seen in the Barri Gòtic, particularly at Plaça de Ramon de Berenguer el Gran (6, C6) and by the northern end of C/del Sotstinent Navarro (4, F9).

Walking on art: Mosaic de Miró (p. 41)

🕐 June-Sept 9am-8.30pm, Apr & May 10am-7.30pm, Oct-Mar 10am-6.30pm (closed for lunch Mon-Fri 1.30-3.30pm outside summer) ⑤ €1.50 ♿

Palau de la Generalitat (6, D3)

This seat of Catalan government was adapted from several Gothic mansions in the early 15th century and extended over time as it grew in importance. It has a Gothic side facade on C/del Bisbe Irurita, which features a wonderful relief of St George made in 1418 by Pere Joan. Its grand interior can only be visited at limited times.

✉ Plaça de Sant Jaume, Barri Gòtic
☎ 93 402 46 00
🌐 www.gencat.es
Ⓜ Jaume I 🕐 free guided tours 2nd and 4th Sun of month at 10.30am (bring ID) ⑤ free ♿ good

Palau Quadras (5, F2)

This building, remodelled by Puig i Cadafalch between 1902 and 1904, now houses the **Museu de la Música** (p. 34), and has fine stained glass and detailed neo-Gothic carvings on its facade.
✉ Avda Diagonal 373, L'Eixample Ⓜ Diagonal

Pavelló Mies van der Rohe (3, J3)

This is a replica of a structure erected for – and demolished with – the World Exhibition in 1929. In hindsight it was considered to be a milestone of modern architecture and was rebuilt in 1986. It is Mies van der Rohe's vision of a new urban environment, with a light and airy design comprising horizontal planes. His famous 'Barcelona chair' was designed for the Germany Pavilion.
✉ Avda Marquès de Comillas, Montjuïc
☎ 93 423 40 16
🌐 www.miesbcn.com
Ⓜ Espanya 🕐 Mon-Sat 10am-8pm ⑤ €2.50 ♿ good

Poble Espanyol (1, A1)

A bit of an imposter in this section, this 'Spanish Village' was put together for the 1929 World Exhibition and comprises replicas of famous buildings and traditional architecture from all over Spain. For a tourist trap, it's quite engaging but its craft shops, restaurants and bars all share the distinction of being overpriced.
✉ Avda Marquès de Comillas, Montjuïc
☎ 93 325 78 66
🌐 www.poble-espanyol.com
Ⓜ Espanya 🕐 Mon 9am-8pm, Tues-Thur 9am-2am, Fri & Sat 10am-4am, Sun 9am-midnight ⑤ €6 ♿ good

Torre de Collserola (2, A3)

This 288m telecommunications tower, designed by Britain's Sir Norman Foster, was built to bring the 1992 Olympics to television viewers around the world. A glass lift shoots up to an observation deck at 115m which affords splendid views of Tibidabo and the city or a less remarkable haze – depending on your luck on the day.
✉ Parc de Collserola, Tibidado 🚂 FCG Av Tibidabo, then Tramvia Blau, then Funicular de Tibidabo ☎ 93 406 93 54 🕐 Wed-Fri 11am-2.30pm & 3.30-7pm, Sat & Sun 11am-7pm (until 8pm in summer) ⑤ €3 ♿

QUIRKY BARCELONA

Ceramiques Pahissa

(6, E4) Catalans have long been renowned for their partiality to poo and scatological humour. In this cute little shop – founded in 1934 and run by a bashful middle-aged couple – among the usual tiles depicting still lifes and flowers, you'll find a series portraying nuns, pastors and maidens squatting in idyllic country locations and dropping enormous turds.

✉ Bda de la Llibreteria 18, Barri Gòtic
☎ 93 315 00 58
Ⓜ Jaume I
🕐 Mon-Sat 10am-2pm & 4.30-8.30pm

Museu del Calçat

(6, C2) Hot foot it to this unexpected treat, the little museum of shoes: dainty ones, famous ones, weird ones, Roman ones, silk ones, seamless ones, baby ones and one gigantic one made for the **Monument a Colom** (p. 43) when it was married to the Statue of Liberty.

✉ Plaça Sant Felip Neri, Barri Gòtic ☎ 93 301 45 33 Ⓜ Jaume I
🕐 Tues-Sun 11am-2pm
💲 €1.20 ♿

Museu de l'Erótica

(4, E6) Falling somewhere between titillation, tawdriness and art, this private collection is devoted to sex and sexuality through the ages. The decor is pseudo seedy, and the diverse exhibits range from exquisite kama sutra illustrations, tribal carvings and Mapplethorpe photos to early porno movies, S&M apparatus and a

6ft wooden penis.
✉ La Rambla 96
☎ 93 318 98 65
🅴 www.erotica museum.com Ⓜ Liceu
🕐 10am-10pm (until midnight in summer)
💲 €7/6

Museu de Carrosses Fúnebres

(3, D9) A fascinating collection of horse-drawn funeral carriages (and a few motorised ones) that were used in the city from the 18th century up until the 1950s. The varying degrees of ornamentation on each indicate the status of the passengers and provide a unique window into the past.

✉ Servies Funeraris building (ask at desk), Sancho de Avila 2, L'Eixample ☎ 93 484 17 20 Ⓜ Marina
🕐 10am-1pm & 4-6pm
💲 free

Museu del Clavegueram

(3, D6) If the stench of the streets is not enough for you, you're cordially invited to engage in some scatological surveying by way of exhibits outlining the history of sewers and a tour of some genuine working drains.

✉ Pg de Sant Joan 98, L'Eixample ☎ 93 457 65 50 Ⓜ Verdaguer
🕐 (unreliable) Tues-Sat 10am-1pm & 4-6pm, Sat & Sun 10am-2pm
💲 free

La Fira

(3, E4) This bizarre booze boutique is furnished entirely from the disused scraps of funfairs and doubles as one of the weirdest museums in town. Don't be thrown by

the wobbling mirrors – have a swig and swing and enjoy the ride.

✉ C/de Provença 171, L'Eixample Ⓜ Diagonal or Hospital Clínic
🕐 Mon-Sat 10.30pm-3am (until 4.30am Fri & Sat) 💲 free

Temple Romà d'Augusti

(6, D4) You'd think nothing to walk past it but inside this courtyard you can see four Corinthian columns of Barcelona's main Roman temple, built in the 1st century, which now support a block of apartments.

✉ C/del Paradis 10, Barri Gòtic Ⓜ Jaume I
🕐 (unreliable) Tues-Sat 10am-2pm & 4-8pm
💲 free

Tours Culturals Tourmix (4)

During the many holidays, look out for this hilarious free city-sponsored show on La Rambla, which consists of a guide and his eager but dim-witted assistant offering 'alternative' cultural tours to locals, all the while poking gentle fun at us tourists.

✉ La Rambla Ⓜ Liceu
🕐 hols only

Martin Hughes

BARCELONA FOR CHILDREN

Barcelona is a fairytale city with all sorts of weird and wonderful stuff the kids won't have seen before. From the street artists of La Rambla to the madcap designs of Modernista buildings, the city is awash with ageless pleasures. As well as the specific child-friendly sights listed on these pages, you could try the Museu Marítim (p. 25), the Museu del Futbol Club Barcelona (p. 15), Torre de Collserola (p. 44), the Museu d'Història de Catalunya (p. 35), a splash on the Golondrinas boats (p. 56), a giddy ride in Telefèric de Montjuïc (cable car; 1, A5) or a visit to any of the beaches and parks. Ask at your hotel for the nearest playground and at the tourist office for details of the **Estiu als Museu** (Summer in the Museums) project. The Centre de Cultura Contemporània de Barcelona (CCCB; p. 33) also has regular kid's programmes. Look for the ☂ icon listed with individual reviews in the Places to Eat, Entertainment and Places to Stay chapters for more kid-friendly options.

La Font Màgica (3, J3)
Delightfully over the top, the biggest of Montjuïc's famous fountains splashes into life with an irresistible summer evening extravaganza of music and light.

Whether it's to the tune of Tchaikovsky or Abba, the waterworks will make you giddy with glee.
✉ **Plaça d'Espanya, Sants** Ⓜ **Plaça d'Espanya** ☺ June-Sept
Thur-Sun (and evenings before public hols) every half hour 9.30-11.30pm ⑤ free

L'Aquàrium (4, K9)
Always a winner with the kids, this ultra-modern aquarium is said to be Europe's best collection of Mediterranean marine life. Highlights include an 80m-long shark tunnel, lots of touch-and-feel activities and a three-level interactive centre, Planeta Aqua, featuring everything from piranhas to penguins.
✉ **Moll d'Espanya, Port Vell** ☎ **93 221 74 74** ℮ **www.aquarium bcn.com**
Ⓜ **Barceloneta**
☺ Jul & Aug 9.30am-11pm, Sept-June Mon-Fri 9.30am-9pm, Sat & Sun 9.30am-9.30pm
⑤ €9.30/5.70
🚻 excellent

Barcelo-little-uns
If you don't see many child facilities around it's because kids are usually treated like little adults in Barcelona. While parents don't drag them out for nights on the razzle, it is common to see toddlers out with mums and dads in restaurants until 11pm or so. Rest assured, your kids will be made to feel welcome wherever you go.

Juggling the needs of the kids is easy in Barcelona.

Museu de Cera (4, H6)
With a collection of 300 wax figures of famous Catalans and familiar faces from around the world, this is just as creepy as any

Take shelter at the Parc Zoològic.

other wax museum although the kids may take a shine to it.

✉ Passatge de la Banca 7, La Rambla ☎ 93 317 26 49 Ⓜ Drassanes ◷ Jul-Sept 10am-8pm Oct-June 10am-1.30pm & 4-7.30pm ⑤ €6.50/3.75

Museu de la Ciencia (2, A5)

An engaging interactive science museum and planetarium where you get to twiddle knobs, press buttons and discover how the world around you works, all the while pretending you're only doing it for the kids. Bear in mind, though, that it's a bit tricky getting here ✉ Teodor Roviralta 55, Zona Alta ☎ 93 212 60 50 ⓡ FGC Tibidabo, then Tramvia Blau ◷ Tues-Sun 10am-8pm ⑤ €3 ♿ excellent

Museu de la Xocolata (4, D11)

Explore the history and potential of chocolate through audio-visual displays (in English on request), touchscreen presentations, historical exhibits and stacks of chocolate models including a very impressive Tintin and

his dog minus a few chunks. There are also cooking demonstrations, tastings and (with advance notice) workshops where the kids can make their own models.

✉ Antic Convent de Sant Agust, Plaça de Pons i Clerch, La Ribera ☎ 93 268 78 78 Ⓜ Jaume I ⑤ €3.50

Parc d'Atraccions

(2, A3) For the Ferris wheel ride of your life – with panoramic views from the top of Tibidabo mountain – head to this cherished old-fashioned funfair, which has all the usual thrills as well as a remarkable Museu d'Autòmats del Tibidabo where you can see carnival games and gizmos dating back to the 19th century.

✉ Plaça del Tibidabo, Tibidabo ☎ 93 211 79 42 ⓡ FGC Tibidabo, then Tramvia Blau and Funicular ◷ varies ⑤ €7.20 (free for kids under 1.1m tall) for entrance, museum and six rides

Parc Zoològic (4, F14)

As thrilling or depressing as any other, this small zoo occupies the southern end of Parc de la Ciutadella and is best known as the home of Snowflake, the only albino gorilla in the world. Orphaned by poachers in Guinea in the 1960s, camera-mugging Snowflake has become something of a symbol for the zoo and the city's rejuvenation.

✉ Parc de la Ciutadella, La Ribera ☎ 93 225 67 80 Ⓜ Ciutadella Vila Olímpica ◷ 10am-7.30pm (to 5pm in winter) ⑤ €9.50 ♿ good

Baby-Sitting & Childcare

Many of the larger hotels provide child-minding facilities and even medium-size hotels often have arrangements with regular carers or can suggest someone reliable. There is usually a three- or four-hour minimum but most are happy to come to your hotel. **Canguir Serveis** (☎ 93 487 80 08 or 24hr mobile 639 66 16 06) is a specialist service that can provide baby-sitters, even at short notice, for about €6.50/hour while **Happy Parc** (Comtes de Bell.lloc 74, Sants; ☎ 93 490 08 35) is a reliable drop-in centre for nippers aged from two to 12.

KEEPING FIT

There are plenty of opportunities for exercise in this healthy, sports-keen city. For information on what you can do where, contact the city council's sports information service, the **Servei d'Informació Esportiva** (Avda de l'Estadi 30-40; ☎ 93 402 30 00; Mon-Fri 8.30am-3pm), which is in the same complex as the Piscines Bernat Picornell (1, B1) on Montjuïc.

Cycling

Barcelona isn't the best spot for casual bike-riding but the tourist office can suggest some suitable routes where you can avoid the hills, pollution and inconsiderate drivers. Bikes, tandems and four-wheelers can be hired from **Los Filicletos** at Pg de Picasso 40 (4, E12; ☎ 93 319 78 11), near Parc de la Ciutadella.

Golf

If you're a golfer, you'll be itching to play in Spain, one of the capitals of the game. Your best option is the course upon which a teenage Seve Ballesteros made his professional debut, the venerable **Club de Golf Sant Cugat** (C/Villa s/n, Sant Cugat del Valles, Outer Limits; ☎ 93 674 39 58; ▣ FGC Sant Cugat). Built in 1919 – a good omen for those who like a round of golf before they start drinking – this attractive course is only moderately difficult and welcomes visitors. Green fees (€55 Mon-Fri, €120 Sat & Sun) entitle you to use of clubs, trolleys, the restaurant, pool and, of course, the 19th. It opens 7.30am to 9pm.

Gym

There are stacks of gyms around the city and most have flexible rates for out-of-towners. Cheapest are those run by the city council – you can get the details from the Servei d'Informació Esportiva. The gym chain **Centres de Fitness DIR** has reasonable guest rates and you can locate their nearest centre by calling ☎ 901 30 40 30.

Jogging

For an easy run and a few gasps of fresh sea air, use the seafront stretch from Vila Olímpica (3, E10) to Barceloneta (3, G8). For a more strenuous stint, keep going up towards Montjuïc.

Skating & Blading

The promenades along the shore-line are your best bet for an

Make the right turn...

obstacle-free blade. You can hire equipment and get some useful routes from **Al Punt de Trobada** at C/de Badajoz 24 (3, D10; ☎ 93 225 15 85; Mon-Fri 9am-2pm & 4-9pm, Sat & Sun 4-10pm), near Vila Olímpica, for around €5/hr. There are regular gatherings outside the Catedral on Thursday evenings around 11pm.

Swimming

If the beaches don't appeal, there are dozens of municipal pools spread around the city, including the rather forlorn-looking Piscines Bernat Picornell at Avda de L'Estadi 30-40 in Montjuïc (1, B1;

> ### Skinny-Dipping
> If the Med is too cold and you're craving to float your wobbly bits, Montjuïc's Piscines Bernat Picornell has a naturist's session on Saturday mornings (9-11am).

☎ 93 423 40 41; Ⓜ Paral.lel, then Funicular de Montjuïc), where the 1992 Olympics were held. It opens 7am to midnight during the week and 7.30am to 9pm at the weekend and costs €8/3 for use of the gym and pool.

Tennis

Check with the Servei d'Informació Esportiva to locate your most convenient court if you've brought your own gear. Otherwise, follow the Olympic trail out to **Barcelona Tens Olímpic** (Pg de la Vall d'Hebron 178-196; ☎ 93 427 65 00; ⓔ bto@fctennis.org; Ⓜ Montbau) where you can hire rackets, buy balls and play on your choice of clay or asphalt. Courts are available from 8am to 11pm (closes at 9pm on Saturday and 7pm on Sunday) and cost €14/hr.

Watersports

For fun in the water, head to Port Olímpic (3, F10) where there are lots of clubs and facilities. Whether you're a giddy splasher or an accomplished sailor, **Base Nautica de la Mar Bella** at Avda Litoral s/n (3, D12; ☎ 93 221 04 32; ⓔ www.basenautica.net; Ⓜ Poble Nou) is the place to come for your aqua apparatus. It's got everything from snorkelling and windsurfing gear to a range of different boats, and offers sailing lessons for beginners. You'll find it on the third beach north after Port Olímpic, it opens 9.30am to 9pm (closes at 6pm in winter).

Martin Hughes

Roll on!

out & about

WALKING TOURS
Barri Gòtic

Facing the Catedral ❶, take the right flank along C/del Bisbe Irurita until you reach the city's administrative heart, Plaça de Sant Jaume ❷. Turn right along C/del Call, the main street of an ancient Jewish quarter known as The Call ❸. At No 5, above the jewellery shop, are remnants of the Roman wall and the south-western gate. A block north up C/de Ramon del Cal, at No 1 C/de Marlet, a graffiti-daubed inscription records the death of a rabbi in AD692. Follow this street and head left into De Santo Domingo del Call and a quick right and left into C/de Sant Felip Neri and the church ❹ and plaça of the same name. Through the arch on C/de Montjuïc del Bisbe turn left to retrace a few steps on C/Bisbe and cross the face of the Catedral to the far side. At Plaça de Sant Iu follow your instinct to descend to the arches of Museu de Frederic Marès ❺ and a tranquil courtyard cafe. Resume along C/dels Comtes de Barcelona, taking the next left on Bda de Santa Clara, where you will be drawn into Plaça del Rei ❻. Note the Museu d'Història de la Ciutat ❼ where you can try an underground version of the walk you've just finished.

Martin Hughes

distance 1km **duration** 1hr
► **start** Ⓜ Jaume I (Avda de la Catedral)
● **end** Ⓜ Jaume I (Plaça del Rei)

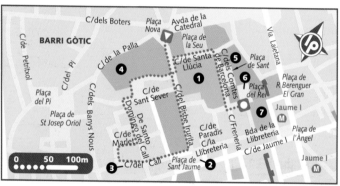

La Ribera

Cross Via Laietana to C/de la Boria, the untouristed part of the old town and the commercial centre of medieval Barcelona. You pass C/de Mercades ('traders') on your left before entering the atmospheric Plaça de la Llana where wool was sold. The street becomes C/dels Corders ('rope makers') and leads to the neglected Capella d'En Marcús ❶. Turn right from C/dels Assaonadors ('tanners') into the grand avenue of C/de Montcada, lined with the mansions of successful merchants from this age, several of which house the Museu Picasso ❷ and the Museu Tèxtil i d'Indumentària ❸. Emerge into Pg del Born ❹, the hip precinct *del dia* (of the day), abutted by the imposing Mercat del Born ❺. Turning right (after an unguided wander) follow the flank of the extraordinarily beautiful Església de Santa Maria del Mar ❻ to an evocative plaça where you should pop into La Vinya del Senyor ❼ for a flute or two of cava. After visiting the church, explore the artisan workshops for which this area is renowned ❽. You could walk back to Plaça de l'Àngel along C/de l'Argenteria ('silver') but it's more rewarding to ramble through the grubby, narrow streets to its right, peppered with ateliers and retail gems.

SIGHTS & HIGHLIGHTS

Capella d'En Marcús (p. 37)
Museu Picasso (p. 28)
Museu Tèxtil i d'Indumentària (p. 37)
Pg del Born
Mercat del Born (p. 43)
Església de Santa Maria del Mar (p. 37)
artisan workshops (p. 62)

Martin Hughes

Detail of Església de Santa Maria del Mar

distance 1.4km **duration** 1½hrs
▶ **start** Ⓜ Jaume I
● **end** Ⓜ Jaume I

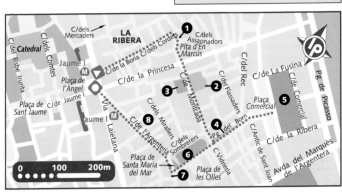

Modernista Tour

Head up Pg de Gràcia with the Manzana de la Discordia ❶ on your left, La Pedrera ❷ a few blocks up on your right and elegant Gaudí-designed lampposts on the way. Right onto Avda Diagonal is Casa Comalat ❸ by Salvador Valeri, which has a more playful facade at the back. The forlorn-looking Palau Quadras, opposite, is an early work by Puig i Cadafalch, and houses the Museu de la Música ❹. Further along is his Casa de les Punxes (House of Spikes) ❺. Drop down C/de Roger de Llúria, detouring left along C/de Mallorca to Casa Thomas, now home to the design showrooms of Bd Ediciones de

Casa de les Punxes (House of Spikes)

Martin Hughes

Diseño ❻. Retake C/de Roger de Llúria down to a burst of Modernisme at the intersection with C/de Valencia: the needle-top Casa Villanueva, the stained-glass Casa Jaume Forn and the Murrià family's shop ❼. Continue down C/de Roger de Llúria several blocks before turning left into C/d'Ausiàs Marc. On the next corner is Farmàcia Nordbeck, a fine example of a Modernist pharmacy ❽. Two extraordinary buildings on the next block are Casa Antoni Roger (built by Enric Sagnier in 1890) ❾ and, further along on the opposite side, Casa Antonia Burés (built by Juli Batllevell in 1906) ❿. Backstep, drop down C/de Girona and right into C/de Sant Pere més Alt until you reach the crowning glory of Modernisme, Palau de la Música Catalana ⓫, before retiring to Els Quatre Gats ⓬.

distance 5.5km **duration** 3hrs
▶ **start** Ⓜ Catalunya
● **end** Ⓜ Urquinaona

El Raval

Incorporating what's left of the once notorious Barri Xinès (Barrio Chino or Chinatown), this walk isn't for the easily unnerved. Starting at the marvellous Museu Marítim ❶, head west along Avda de les Drassanes into the heart of Barri Xinès and turn right into the narrow and atmospheric C/de l'Arc de Teatre, which used to be famous for its brothels, patronised by many of the city's famous sons. Spill left onto La Rambla and left again into C/Nou de la Rambla, the main thoroughfare of this seedy quarter. Pass Gaudí's Palau Güell ❷ on your left and clusters of prostitutes

distance 3km **duration** 2hrs
▶ **start** Ⓜ Drassanes
● **end** Ⓜ Universitat

Damien Simons

Roof of Antic Hospital de la Santa Creu

and transvestites at every intersection until you (almost) reach Avda del Paral.lel where clubs such as the legendary Bagdad maintain the precinct's reputation for staging the bawdiest sex shows. Turn right at C/de l'Abat Safont and right again into C/de Sant Pau, where you'll find the city's oldest surviving Romanesque church, Església de Sant Pau del Camp ❸. After the Modernista marvel of the Hotel Espanya ❹ turn left into C/de l'Arc de Sant Agustí and through the tranquil grounds of Antic Hospital de la Santa Creu ❺ to emerge on C/del Carme. Turning left and then right onto C/dels Àngels will lead you, via a stop off for refreshments at the elegant Silenus ❻, to the gleaming and relatively new Museu d'Art Contemporani de Barcelona ❼.

EXCURSIONS

Teatre-Museu Dalí (7, B5)

Since you're in Barcelona, you may as well visit the doyen of daftness, Mister Salvador Dalí. The spiritual centre of Europe (as Dalí liked to call it) is an extraordinary museum created by the surrealist in Figueres, the town of his birth. It comprises three floors of tricks, illusions and absurdity where even the catalogue is designed to confuse. The final exhibit, and the plainest one by far, is Dalí's tomb, where he has been encased since 1989 (probably dead). Apart from the opportunity to traipse through one of the most fertile imaginations of the 20th century, there's not much else to this town.

INFORMATION

100km north-east of Barcelona

🚆 RENFE from Estació Sants (2¼hrs)

✉ Plaça Gala-Salvador Dalí 5, Figueres

☎ 972 67 75 00

ⓘ tourist office ☎ 972 50 31 55

🕐 July-Sept: Tues-Sun 9am-8pm; Oct-June: Tues-Sun 10.30am-6pm

💲 €7

Painted ceiling at the Teatre-Museu Dalí

Montserrat (7, C3)

Montserrat (Serrated Mountain) is the spiritual heart of Catalunya and your best opportunity to enjoy awesome scenery on a day trip from Barcelona. Comprising a remarkable massif of limestone pinnacles rising precipitously over deep gorges, it is a wondrous place that has drawn hermits (er, independent travellers) since the 5th century. Perched on a dramatic cliff is a monastery and a 12th-century chapel built to house **La Moreneta** (The Black Virgin), a statue found nearby and venerated by hundreds of thousands of people each year. But it's the setting that makes Montserrat so worthwhile and the cable cars, which connect various points of the mountain, provide the perfect platform from which to enjoy it.

INFORMATION

50km north-west of Barcelona

🚆 FGC Espanya to Montserrsat-Aeri (1hr; €17); all-in-one ticket includes return train, cable cars and metro rides

🚌 Julià company (☎ 93 490 40 00) departs Estació d'Autobusos de Sants at 9am (8am in Jul & Aug); return fare €8.50,

ⓘ information office (☎ 93 877 77 77; 10am-6pm) above cable car station; good free leaflet available

Monestir de Montserrat

Sitges   (7, D3)

Only half an hour from Barcelona, Sitges is a unique resort that in summer attracts hordes of fashionable city folk and a huge international gay set. It was a trendy hang-out for artists and bohemians in the 1890s and has remained one of Spain's most unconventional resorts ever since. It's no less attractive in winter although you won't have much company as you cavort between museums (including the **Museu Romàntic**, which has hundreds of antique dolls), admire the sun-bleached baroque church that stands on a promontory over the beach, soak in the fishing village atmosphere and wonder if it's too cold for a dip at the nudie beach.

Caves Codorníu (7, D3)

For a day of sipping bubbles and breathing fresh country air, head to the Penedès, one of Spain's premier wine-growing regions and where virtually all of its cava (sparkling wine) is produced. The capital of cava production is Sant Sadurní d'Anoia, 45mins south-west of Barcelona. Enjoy tastings and a tour at Caves Codorníu, a pioneer of the industry that first began bottling in 1872. It is housed in a magnificent Modernista building and has the world's largest wine cellar. Alternatively, if you have you own wheels and fancy exploring more of the region, get a list of wineries from the tourist office in **Vilafranca del Penedès** (55km, same directions as for Caves Codorníu) before you set out. The tourist office is at Plaça de la Vila (☎ 93 892 03 58; Tues-Fri 9am-1pm & 4-7pm, Sat 10am-1pm).

INFORMATION

41km south-west of Barcelona

🚆 RENFE from Estació Sants or Passeig de Gràcia (€2.10, 30mins, every 20mins)

☎ 93 894 42 51 (tourist office)

ⓔ www.sitgestur.com

Bethune Carmichael

Fun in the sun at Sitges...

INFORMATION

44km south-west of Barcelona

🚆 RENFE from Estació Sants to Sant Sadurní d'Anoia

🚗 take the A-2, then the A-7 and follow the signs

✉ Avda Jaume Codorníu, Sant Sadurní d'Anoia

☎ 93 818 32 32

ⓔ www.codorniu.es

ⓘ visit includes train ride through the cellars, short video presentation, tasting and free glass of cava

🕐 Mon-Fri 9am-5pm, Sat & Sun 9am-1pm

💲 €1.50

ORGANISED TOURS

Turisme de Barcelona, in the basement of Plaça de Catalunya 17 (4, A7; ☎ 906 30 12 82; **e** www.barcelonaturisme.com), offers a range of organised tours and can supply information on others. For the inside track without the company, you can tailor your own tour through the **Barcelona Guide Bureau** (4, B8; Via Laietana 54; ☎ 93 268 24 22; **e** www.bgb.es). Guides charge between €140 and €190 for up to four hours.

Barcelona by Bicycle
(4, F11) The bicycle store Un Cotxe Menys (One Car Less) organises day and evening bike tours around the old quarters and shoreline. Wheels and snacks included.
⊠ C/de l'Espartería 3, La Ribera ☎ 93 268 21 05 **e** www.bicicleta barcelona.com ⊘ shop Mon-Fri 10am-2pm ⑤ day tours €15; evening €36 (incl dinner)

Bus Turístic (4, A7)
These hop-on, hop-off double-decker buses run on two routes, north and south of the city, delivering tourists to most of the worthy sights. They are very handy if you're tight on time and you can purchase tickets on board.
⊠ Tourist Office, Plaça de Catalunya 17, L'Eixample ☎ 906 30 12 82 ⊘ July-Sept every 10mins; Oct-Jun every 30mins ⑤ one day €13.50/8; two days €17

Golondrinas (4, H8)
A swallow boat trip to and from the lighthouse takes 35mins while a longer outing goes to Port Olímpic in a glass-bottomed catamaran. A full schedule runs from June to September; otherwise call to check as the schedule depends on demand outside these months.
⊠ Moll de la Fusta, Port Vell ☎ 93 442 31 06 **e** www.lasgolon drinas.com ⊘ summer 11am-8pm (call for times) ⑤ lighthouse €3.50; Port Olímpic €8

Julià Tours (4, A5)
Guided coach tours around the city and to far-flung parts of Catalunya. One worthy excursion, the 'Visita Ciudad Artística', focuses on the artistic significance of Barcelona.
⊠ Ronda de la Universitat 5, L'Eixample ☎ 93 317 64 54 ⊘ Mon-Sat 9am-6pm ⑤ approx €29 half-day to €65 full day

Museu d'Història Walks (6, D5)
The Museu d'Història de la Ciutat organises terrific tours through the museum and the atmospheric buildings around Plaça del Rei. Nit al Museu, the evening tour, is the best.
⊠ C/Veguer 2, Barri Gòtic ☎ 93 315 11 11 ⊘ call for details ⑤ average €6

My Favourite Things
There is no better way to see Barcelona than with these wonderful alternative walking tours – ranging from gourmet delis to artisan workshops and Barcelona for kids – which open many doors that would otherwise be firmly closed to tourists. Katrien, the 'babbling Belgian dwarf', is an energetic guide and can tailor the tours to whatever you fancy.
☎ 93 329 53 51 or 637 265 405 **e** www.myft .net ⑤ €27-54 ⚹

Pullmantur (3, A6)
A range of options from quick city surveys to full day tours of Girona and the kooky world of Dalí in Figueres.
⊠ Gran Vía de les Corts Catalánes 645, L'Eixample ☎ 93 317 12 97 ⊘ Mon-Sat 10am-7pm ⑤ approx €29 half-day to €65 full day

Turisme de Barcelona Walking Tour (4, A7)
An excellent introduction to the history of the Barri Gòtic with an English-speaking guide. It takes about 90mins but you'll want to return to every place. Numbers are limited so booking is advisable.
⊠ Tourist Office, Plaça de Catalunya 17, L'Eixample ☎ 906 30 12 82 ⊘ Sat & Sun 10am ⑤ €6/3

shopping

It may not have been the lure of shopping that brought you to Barcelona, but it will be one of the reasons you come back. The tourist office claims that Barcelona has the highest number of shops per person in Europe, but it's the quality that impresses most. From tiny specialist stores to mammoth malls, Barcelona is a retail revelation with ample opportunity to send your bank manager into a tizz. Whether it's need or desire that drives your spree – or the realisation that your wardrobe is dowdy compared to the locals – you'll find good value and plenty of choice. And with everyone sharing hearty *holas* when you walk through the door, shopping in Barcelona is as sociable as it is fun.

Barri Gòtic is one of the best precincts, with groovy street, club and second-hand wear mingling with antique shops and engaging junk. But it's the quirky specialist stores, some of which have been plying the same trade for more than a century, that make it buzz. The parallel boulevards of Rambla de Catalunya and Pg de Gràcia in **l'Eixample** are lined with local and international boutiques and jewellery stores. **La Ribera** abounds in artisan workshops while **El Raval** is becoming an increasingly interesting browse as design and fashion outlets spring up to contrast with the clutch of alternative clothes and music retailers on the inimitable C/de la Riera Baixa.

Opening Times

Most places have retail windows between 10am and 1pm and 4pm and 8pm. Traditional shops always observe the siesta while modern ones, and those on main shopping streets, often stay open throughout the day. Virtually all shops are closed on Sunday.

In fact, Barcelona's shopping is so tempting that you may find yourself making an emergency purchase: a new bag to bring all your gear home.

Travelling light to Barcelona will give you the perfect excuse to shop till you drop.

Martin Hughes

ANTIQUES & CRAFTS

Bulevard dels Antiquaris (5, H2)

Part of the Bulevard Rosa shopping mall, this stretch is crammed with more than 70 antique shops tempting you with the this-and-that of old. A few specialists to look out for include Brahuer (jewellery), Trik-Trak (old tin toys), Govary's (porcelain dolls), Dalmau (wooden picture frames) and Victory (crystal).

✉ Pg de Gràcia 55, L'Eixample ☎ 93 215 44 99 Ⓜ Passeig de Gràcia ◷ Mon-Sat 9.30am-1.30pm & 4.30-8.30pm (closed Sat in winter)

Centre Català d'Artesania (5, H2)

For a look at the latest in high-quality crafts, pop into this store dedicated to preserving and promoting Catalunya's craft-making traditions.

✉ Pg de Gràcia 55, L'Eixample ☎ 93 467 46 60 Ⓜ Passeig de Gràcia ◷ Mon-Sat 10am-8pm

Gotham (4, F7)

The best retro shop in Barcelona specialises in furniture and furnishings from the 1950s, '60s and

Antique treasures await you behind many a door.

'70s but you'll also find a mix of older stuff and up-to-the-minute new designs.

✉ C/de Cervantes 7, Barri Gòtic ☎ 93 412 46 47 Ⓜ Jaume I ◷ Mon-Sat 10.30am-2pm & 5-8.30pm

Gothsland Galeria d'Art (5, J1)

Probably not the take-home variety of antiques but this place stocks a unique and enlightening collection of Modernista furniture, art and decorations.

✉ C/del Consell de Cent 331, L'Eixample ☎ 93 488 19 22 Ⓜ Passeig de Gràcia ◷ Mon-Sat 10am-1.30pm & 4.30-8pm

La Llar del Col.leccionisme

(6, D4) The friendly 'Home of Collecting' has an enthralling collection of small bric-a-brac items such as medals, pendants and old postcards.

✉ C/la Llibreteria 13, Barri Gòtic ☎ 93 268 32 59 Ⓜ Jaume I ◷ Mon-Fri 10am-1.30pm & 4.30-8.30pm, Sat 10am-1.30pm

Tombbus

The T1 *Tombbus* bus route was set up for shoppers and runs from Plaça de Catalunya up along Avda Diagonal taking in many department stores and the more mainstream shopping precincts. It operates from 7.30am to 9.30pm Monday to Saturday and costs €1.10. The name means 'round trip' and isn't necessarily an invitation to retail yourself into an early grave.

BOOKS

Altair (5, H1)

If you need any encouragement in planning your next trip, these travel specialists will give you a nudge in the right direction. There's an impressive range of local interest books as well as guides, maps and knowledgeable staff.

✉ C/de Balmes 71, L'Eixample ☎ 93 454 29 66 Ⓜ Passeig de Gràcia ⏰ Mon-Sat 10am-2pm & 4.30-8pm

Come In (5, G1)

If you read and think in English, this is about the best bookshop in the city. It has a decent selection of general interest material as well as professional manuals and reference titles.

✉ C/de Provença 203, L'Eixample ☎ 93 453 12 04 Ⓜ Hospital Clínic ⏰ Mon-Sat 10am-2pm & 4.30-8pm

Cómplices (4, F7)

Gay Barcelona's original bookshop is run by a friendly women's group and has two levels of books, videos, postcards, T-shirts, cards and games. There is a decent selection of books in English downstairs and this is a reliable place to get your map of gay Barcelona.

✉ C/de Cervantes 2, Barri Gòtic ☎ 93 412 72 83 ⒺΙ www.personal1 .iddeo.es/complices Ⓜ Jaume I ⏰ Mon-Fri 10.30am-8.30pm, Sat noon-8.30pm

El Lokal (4, E2)

For anyone with a social conscience, this shop

Three Books on Barcelona

For a fascinating insight into what makes Catalunya's capital unique, there is no better read than Robert Hughes' *Barcelona*, a passionate study of the art, architecture, history and character of the city. George Orwell's first-hand account of the Spanish Civil War, and its impact on Barcelona, *Homage to Catalonia*, is an enthralling examination of a tragic chapter in Spain's history, while Colm Tóibín's *Homage to Barcelona* is a wonderful anecdotal introduction to Barcelona's modern and artistic life.

---

stocks a comprehensive range of books on how to buck the establishment. There are also general titles for those who care less and a section devoted to CDs, videos, T-shirts and magazines that you won't see in shop windows.

✉ C/de la Cera 1, El Raval ☎ 93 329 06 43 Ⓜ Sant Antoni ⏰ Mon-Sat 10am-2pm & 5-9pm (evenings only Mon & Sat)

Laie (5, K4)

A leisure complex for the mind, this bookshop combines a broad range of books with a splendid cafe, an international outlook and accommodating staff.

✉ C/de Pau Claris 85, L'Eixample ☎ 93 518 17 39 ⒺΙ www.laie.es Ⓜ Urquinaona ⏰ Mon-Sat 10am-8pm

Próleg (4, E8)

More like a club than a bookshop, this store is run by women for women and concentrates on feminist titles as well as organising activities such as writing workshops and forums.

✉ C/de la Dagueria 13,

Barri Gòtic ☎ 93 319 24 25 ⒺΙ www.mallorca web.net/proleg Ⓜ Jaume I ⏰ Mon-Sat 10am-2pm & 5-8pm (afternoons only Aug)

Ras (4, C4)

This bright and stylish space is used as a gallery, exhibition centre and bookshop concentrating on contemporary architecture, photography and design.

✉ C/del Doctor Dou 10, El Raval ☎ 93 412 71 99 ⒺΙ www.actar.es Ⓜ Catalunya ⏰ 11am-2pm & 4-8pm (closed first 2 weeks Aug)

Martin Hughes

Let us at those bargains!

DEPARTMENT STORES & MALLS

Bulevard Rosa (5, H2)
With over 100 shops featuring some of the most interesting local designers of fashion and jewellery, this 1980s creation is the best mall in the city for style and a few hours of boutique-browsing.
✉ **Pg de Gràcia 55, L'Eixample** ☎ **93 309 06 50** e **www.bulevard rosa.com**
Ⓜ **Passeig de Gràcia**
🕐 Mon-Sat 10.30am-8.30pm

El Corte Inglés (4, A7)
This monster of retail has everything you could possibly want and lots more that won't have crossed your mind. There's also a rooftop cafe with a splendid view. There are branches around the city at Avda Diagonal 471 (3, E2; ☎ 93 419 20 20), Avda Diagonal 617 (3, E1; ☎ 93 419 28 28) and Avda del Portal de l'Angel 19 (4, B7; ☎ 93 306 38 00).
✉ **Plaça de Catalunya 14, L'Eixample** ☎ **93 306 38 00** e **www .elcorteingles.es**
Ⓜ **Catalunya** 🕐 Mon-Sat 10am-10pm

El Triangle (4, B6)
Occupying an entire corner of Plaça de Catalunya, this new and uninspiring mall is redeemed by some worthy stores including FNAC and Sephora (p. 68).
✉ **C/de Pelai 39, L'Eixample**
☎ **93 318 01 08**
e **www.eltriangle.es**
Ⓜ **Catalunya**
🕐 Mon-Sat 10am-10pm

FNAC (4, B5)
This hugely popular megastore – part of the French-owned chain – specialises in CDs, tapes, videos, books and video games at discount prices. There's a useful ticket desk on the ground floor, which has lists of upcoming events and sells tickets.
✉ **El Triangle, Plaça de Catalunya 4, L'Eixample**
☎ **93 344 18 00**
e **www.fnac.es**
Ⓜ **Catalunya** 🕐 Mon-Sat 10am-10pm

L'Illa (3, D3)
This massive mall in the heart of the business district caters to uptowners and houses swanky designer stores and all the usual chains. The complex is one of the more interesting architectural developments of recent years.
✉ **Avda Diagonal 545, L'Eixample** ☎ **93 444 00 00** e **www.lilla .com** Ⓜ **Maria Cristina**
🕐 Mon-Sat 10am-9.30pm

Maremàgnum (4, K8)
Soulless even by the standards of a normal shopping mall, this glassy modern complex (built on land reclaimed from the sea) houses restaurants, clubs and lots of tourist-orientated gift and souvenir stores.
✉ **Moll d'Espanya, Port Vell** ☎ **93 225 81 00**
e **www.maremagnum .es** Ⓜ **Drassanes**
🕐 11am-11pm

El Corte Inglés

Barcelona Bargains
Serious shoppers plan their sprees around the city's seasonal sales (*rebaixes* in Catalan, *rebajas* in Castilian). Everything is marked down from the middle of January to the end of February and summer styles are practically given away from around 5 July – the perfect opportunity for lucky southern hemisphere visitors to make an absolute killing on their new wardrobe (or to second-guess next year's fashion if you're from the northern hemisphere).

DESIGN, HOMEWARE & GIFTS

Aspectos (4, E11)
When hanging around El Borne, design-buffs should make a little time for this prestigious shop with a broad range of furniture and Art Deco knick-knacks from big name designers and figures of the future.
✉ C/del Rec 28, El Borne ☎ 93 319 52 85 Ⓜ Jaume I ⏲ Mon-Fri 4.30-8pm, Sat 10.30am-2pm (closed Aug)

Bath Time (5, E1)
One of the most stunningly stylish stores in town, this place is devoted to suds and stuff with everything from fixtures to towels.
✉ Avda Diagonal 460, L'Eixample ☎ 93 218 53 77 Ⓜ Diagonal ⏲ Mon-Sat 10.30am-2.30pm & 4.30-8.30pm

Bd Ediciones de Diseño (5, G3)
An awesome shop where you'll find classics of modern furniture design alongside bold and contemporary creations in a Modernista building constructed by Domènech i Montaner in 1895. A must for anyone interested in design or retail atmosphere (although the prices are way out of our league).
✉ C/de Mallorca 291, L'Eixample ☎ 93 458 69 09 🆔 www.bdbarcelona.com Ⓜ Diagonal ⏲ Mon-Sat 10am-2pm & 4-8pm (closed first 3 weeks Aug)

Dom (5, G2)
Retro aesthetics are reworked in 21st-century styles at this little design shop, stacked with everyday furniture, lamps, CDs, magazines, plants, lots of things that can be inflated and far too many 'Don't Touch' signs. There's another branch at C/d'Avinyo 7, Barri Gòtic (4, F7; ☎ 93 342 55 91).
✉ Pg de Gràcia 76, L'Eixample ☎ 93 487 11 81 🆔 www.id-dom.com Ⓜ Passeig de Gràcia ⏲ Mon-Sat 10am-8pm

Dos i Una (5, F4)
Fun is the watchword and style the way at this friendly store, with all the designer accessories, gimmicks and games required to keep kids and adults entertained for hours.
✉ C/de Rosselló 275, L'Eixample ☎ 93 217 70 32 Ⓜ Diagonal ⏲ Mon-Sat 10.30am-2pm & 4.30-8.30pm

Ganiveteria Roca
(4, E6) If it needs to be cut, clipped, snipped, trimmed, shorn, shaved or cropped, you'll find the perfect instrument at this classic gentleman's shop.
✉ Plaça del Pi 3, Barri Gòtic ☎ 93 302 12 41 Ⓜ Liceu ⏲ Mon-Fri 9.45am-1.30pm & 4.15-8pm, Sat 5-8pm

Insolit (3, D6)
The name is the Catalan for 'unusual', an accurate description of the thoroughly original designs to be found here. The surreal and playful furniture, accessories and gadgets are all created by the owners themselves.
✉ Avda Diagonal 353, L'Eixample ☎ 93 207 49 19 Ⓜ Verdaguer ⏲ Mon-Sat 10am-1.30pm & 4.30-8pm

Martin Hughes

Ganiveteria Roca: other gents' stores just don't cut it.

Meet the Makers

For the most memorable and rewarding purchases, adventurous shoppers head to the old quarters and the thriving tradition of workshops and ateliers. Young local and international designers, keen to work in the city's dynamic atmosphere, set up studios and play a large hand in maintaining Barcelona's reputation for cutting-edge design. Very few have permanent showrooms, regular hours or any signage but curious visitors are usually welcome. As you wander the narrow streets of Barri Gòtic and La Ribera in particular, look and listen for workshop activity and don't be afraid to enquire. From jewellery to furniture and glassware to textiles the potential is boundless and you'll usually be able to buy these beautiful and unique designer wares before the museum shops mark them up.

Taller de Lenceria

(5, F4) This is a charming little shop specialising in traditional-design bed clothes made to order and sold off the peg with monograms embroidered while you wait.
✉ C/del Rosselló 271, L'Eixample ☎ 93 415 39 52 Ⓜ Diagonal

🕐 Mon-Sat 10am-1.30pm & 4-7pm

Vinçon (5, F2)

Despite its lofty reputation as the frame in which Spanish design evolves, this superb shop is relaxed and unpretentious. Even if you're not in the market for domestic appliances, furniture and everyday practical items, pamper your aesthetic senses with a journey through its local and imported wares.
An annexe at C/de Rosselló 246, known as Tinc-con (I'm sleepy), has the finest designer linen and beds.
✉ Pg de Gràcia 96, L'Eixample
☎ 93 215 60 50
e www.vincon.com
Ⓜ Passeig de Gràcia
🕐 Mon-Sat 10am-2pm & 4.30-8.30pm

Zoo (4, F7)

Zoo stocks everything from coloured light bulbs and stylish kitchen wares to original must-have pieces from alternative local artists. It will be even better when the licence for their cafe bar out the back comes through.
✉ C/d'Avinyo 22, Barri Gòtic ☎ 93 412 51 86
Ⓜ Jaume I
🕐 Mon-Sat 10.30am-9pm (closed Wed & Thur for lunch)

FASHION, CLOTHES & SHOES

While the fashion of Barcelona – and Spain – had its time in the international spotlight in the early 1990s before it was shoved aside by Belgium's cutting edge, there is still a wonderfully vibrant, diverse and innovative local scene with graduates and old hands pushing each other to lofty levels of design and detail.

Antonio Miró (5, J2)

The doyen of Barcelona couture, Antonio Miró made his name by producing elegant and unpretentious classic fashion of the highest quality for men and women. He launched his career in Groc (5, G1; Rambla de Catalunya 100, ☎ 93 202 30 70) in 1967 and the store is still run by his family and stocks many of his designs. Miró also does an attractive line in accessories.
✉ C/del Consell de Cent 349, L'Eixample
☎ 93 487 06 70
Ⓜ Passeig de Gràcia
🕐 Mon-Sat 10am-2pm & 4.30-8.30pm

Adolfo Domínguez

(5, J2) This Galician is one of Spain's most celebrated designers and was part of the reason the eyes of the fashion world were upon Barcelona in the early 1990s. His designs may have become a little more conservative since those heady days but he still produces timeless fashions for men and women with exquisite tailoring and quality materials.

✉ **Pg de Gràcia 32, L'Eixample** ☎ 93 487 41 70 **e** www.adolfo dominguez.es

Ⓜ **Passeig de Gràcia** ☺ Mon-Sat 10am-8.30pm

Armand Basi (5, H2)

James Bond's long-time outfitter was popular with 'lads about town' some years ago but then seemed to lose track of the market. Its reappearance in prestigious stores all over Europe suggests that Armand is back. This is the only place you'll find the whole dashing collection, from classic knitwear and timeless suits to elegant evening dresses and accessories.

✉ **Pg de Gràcia 49, L'Eixample** ☎ 93 215 14 21 **e** www.armand basi.com Ⓜ **Passeig de Gràcia** ☺ Mon-Sat 10am-8.30pm

Bad Habits (5, H2)

This is a bunker full of ballsy and original fashion for women with the confidence to take a risk. Blurring the lines between feminine and masculine, colour and monochrome, Bad Habits stocks international labels as well as its own line.

✉ **C/de València 261, L'Eixample** ☎ 93 487 22 59 Ⓜ **Passeig de Gràcia** ☺ Mon-Sat 10.30am-2.30pm & 4.30-8.30pm

Bhuno (4, C4)

A classy store stocked with the elegant and city chic creations of Antonio Miró's protege, Barbera Oliveras.

✉ **C/d'Elisabets 18, El Raval** ☎ 93 412 63 05 Ⓜ **Catalunya** ☺ Mon-Sat 10.30am-8.30pm

Camper (4, B5)

This classic Spanish shoe merchant continues to stamp all over the international market by successfully treading the fine line between rebellion and commercial. Outside the sales, you probably won't get any bargains but you get to choose from the entire range, only a fraction of which makes it to your local store. Branches at C/de València 249 (5, H2; ☎ 93 215 63 90), C/de Muntaner 248 (3, D3; ☎ 93 201 31 88) and Rambla de Catalunya 122 (5, F1; ☎ 93 217 23 84).

✉ **El Triangle, C/de Pelai 13-37, L'Eixample** ☎ 93 215 63 90 Ⓜ **Catalunya** ☺ Mon-Sat 10am-10pm

Cool Hunter (4, C7)

Shoes, accessories and sensational clothes live in this cavern of cool where you'll find the reworked vintage labels of Puma Platinum and Levi's-Red, along with trend setters such as D-Squared and Andrew Mackenzie.

✉ **Passatge Duc de la Victòria 5, Barri Gòtic** ☎ 93 302 37 78 Ⓜ **Liceu** ☺ Mon-Fri 11am-2pm & 4.30-8.30pm, Sat 10.30am-9.30pm

Custo Barcelona (4, F11)

Created in the early 1980s by the Dalmau brothers, Custo is currently the biggest name in Barcelona fashion and its trendiest export. It specialises in unique long-sleeve tees, for men and women, with bold and psychedelic graphics that don't just jump out at you, they wrap their beautiful fabrics around your inspecting hand and lead it to your pocket.

✉ **Plaça de les Olles, La Ribera** ☎ 93 268 78 93 **e** www.custo -barcelona.com Ⓜ **Barceloneta** ☺ Mon-Sat 10am-10pm, Sun 1-8pm

Martin Hughes

Get ahead on your street cred with Camper shoes.

E-male (3, F4)

If your dowdy wardrobe is holding you back on the dance floor, it may be time for a Latin make-over. This shop (and a couple of others on this street) stocks the most up-to-the-minute trends in international club wear, most of which require a tan and a very fit bootie.

✉ **C/del Consell de Cent 236, L'Eixample** ☎ **93 454 08 72** Ⓜ **Universitat** ⏲ **Mon-Sat 10.30am-2pm & 5-9pm**

Farrutx (5, G1)

The splendidly sober architecture of this shop is the perfect setting to showcase the wares of Catalunya's finest shoemakers, Farrutx, who have been dressing the heels of Barcelona's uptown women for decades.

✉ **C/de Rosselló 218, L'Eixample** ☎ **93 215 06 85** Ⓜ **Diagonal** ⏲ **Mon-Sat 10am-8.30pm**

Gimenez & Zuazo (4, C4)

Playful twists, vibrant colours and original details on classic themes have placed this duo among the most popular couturiers to stylish urban women.

✉ **C/d'Elisabets 20, El Raval** ☎ **93 412 33 81** Ⓜ **Catalunya** ⏲ **Mon-Sat 10.30am-2pm & 5-8.30pm**

Mango (5, H2)

Begun in Barcelona in the 1980s, Mango has gone massive around the world with its combination of sexy and sassy couture, reliable fabrics and department store prices. Slightly younger and funkier than its main rival, Zara (p. 65), Mango produces originals as well as knock-offs from the big names and is a great place for guys and gals to stretch their euros. There are many branches around town, including at Avda del Portal d'Angel 7 (4, C7; ☎ 93 317 69 85) and C/de Pelai 48 (4, A4; ☎ 93 317 44 83).

✉ **Pg de Gràcia 65, L'Eixample** ☎ **93 215 75 30** Ⓜ **Passeig de Gràcia** ⏲ **Mon-Sat 10.30am-8.30pm**

Modart (3, C3)

Jose Rivero and Carmen Trias are the creators of unique designs for men and women, comprising original comfy garments made with natural fibres in vivacious colours. You won't like everything here but you could also find that one-off that makes you the most popular person at the party.

✉ **C/d'Astúries 34, L'Eixample** ☎ **93 238 07 86** Ⓜ **Fontana**

⏲ **Mon-Sat 11am-2pm & 5-9pm**

On Land (5, G3)

Brimming with bonhomie and casually funky clothing from young and unfettered designers, this store will tempt you into a make-over. The owners have been inspired by their five-year-old daughter to start a kids' range, which you should check if your little princess is the same age. There's another branch at C/de la Princesa 25 (4, D10; ☎ 93 310 02 11).

✉ **C/de València 273, L'Eixample** ☎ **93 215 56 25** Ⓜ **Passeig de Gràcia** ⏲ **Mon-Sat 11am-2pm & 5-8.30pm (closed Mon morning)**

Overales & Bluyines (4, D11)

This relaxed and spacious store has funky international street labels sitting alongside local lines such as Fake London, Divinas Palabras and an exclusive range from the teasingly playful Anaoana,

Not very fruity but certainly very fashionable: Mango

whose handmade and recycled gear is so cute that it won't be exclusive for long. The owner has just started his own line in vivid tees with clever graphics.

✉ C/del Rec 65, El Borne ☎ 93 319 29 76 Ⓜ Barceloneta ◷ Mon-Sat 10.30am-8.30pm (closed Thurs lunch)

Roser-Francesc (5, G3)

Civilised and muted, the men's and women's collections in this store encompass a host of international labels along with local names such as Lydia Delgado, Antonio Miró and Konrad Muhr.

✉ C/de València 285, L'Eixample ☎ 93 459 14 53 Ⓜ Passeig de Gràcia ◷ Mon-Sat 10.30am-2pm & 4.30-8pm

So-Da (4, F7)

So-Da is a groovy little shop with a small but choice selection of street labels, including some wicked old-school Adidas. The back of the shop turns into an equally groovy bar at night with DJs and cocktails.

✉ C/d'Avinyo 24, Barri Gòtic ☎ 93 412 27 76 Ⓜ Jaume I ◷ shop Mon-Sat 11am-2pm & 4.30-9pm, bar Mon-Sat 9pm-3am & Sun 6pm-1am

Spike (4, E5)

You'll find the best selection of denim and street wear at this new shop, energetically run by the new French posse in town. Lots of international labels such as Energie, Diesel and Levi's Engineered for boys, and the likes of Jnco, E-play

Martin Hughes

and Miss Sixty for chix. Nearby **Spike Action**, at Plaça de la Vila de Madrid 5 (4, C6; ☎ 93 412 27 59), is mainly for gay boys and adds undies and swimwear to the range.

✉ C/de l'Hospital 46, El Raval ☎ 93 412 64 67 Ⓜ Liceu ◷ Mon-Sat 11am-2pm & 5-9pm

T4 (4, F7)

This achingly hip shoe shop has an exquisite range of Italian footwear plus classic urban casuals from Gola, Stride and Royal Elastic.

✉ C/d'Avinyo 12, Barri Gòtic ☎ 93 318 65 10 Ⓜ Liceu ◷ Mon-Sat 11am-2pm & 4.30-8.30pm

Tactic (3, F4)

The best shop for surf and skate wear has all the international brands you'd expect from such – Quiksilver, Ripcurl, Mooks DC Shoe Company et al – along with a smattering of indigenous labels from around Spain.

✉ C/Enric Granados 11, L'Eixample ☎ 93 451 03 87 Ⓜ Universitat ◷ Tues-Sat 10.45am-2pm & 5-8pm

Zara (4, B5)

The Spanish name synonymous with inexpensive and good quality smart casuals (that aren't made in sweat shops) has blossomed internationally in recent years, thanks to a carefully commercialised fashion edge. The clothes seem more conservative in their place of origin but you can still save a well groomed arm and a leg by stocking up here. Ignore the make-believe international prices on the labels, ask instead. There are many branches around town.

✉ C/de Pelai 58, L'Eixample ☎ 93 301 09 78 Ⓜ Catalunya ◷ Mon-Sun 10am-9pm

Zinc (4, F7)

Fans of classic street wear will wobble at the knees when they see the range in the local Levis vintage store, which includes wearable art and groovy occasional furniture at collectors' prices.

✉ C/d'Avinyo 14, Barri Gòtic ☎ 93 342 62 88 Ⓜ Liceu ◷ Mon-Sat 10.30am-9pm

FOOD & DRINK

Cafes El Magnifico
(4, F10) Take a veritable tour of world coffee with the friendly Sans family as your guide. They had so much fun with their beans and blends that they opened up another store across the street, **Sans & Sans Colonials** (C/de l'Argenteria 59; ☎ 93 319 60 81) Ⓜ Jaume I), devoted to more than 200 types of tea.
✉ **C/de l'Argenteria 64, La Ribera ☎ 93 339 60 81** Ⓜ **Jaume I**
⏰ **Mon-Sat 8.30am-1.30pm & 4-8pm, Sat 9.30am-1.30pm**

Gispert (4, F10)
Nuts and coffee are roasted in an antique 19th-century wood oven at this wonderfully aromatic wholesaler's. Hazelnuts and almonds are the specialities, complemented by piles of dried fruit and a host of artisan products such as mustards and preserves.
✉ **C/dels Sombreres 23, La Ribera**

La Boqueria market (p. 69)
Martin Hughes

☎ **93 319 75 35**
Ⓜ **Jaume I** ⏰ **Mon-Fri 9am-1.30pm & 4-7.30pm, Sat 10am-2pm & 5-8pm**

Escribà (4, E5)
Chocolates, dainty pastries and mouth-watering cakes can all be lapped up behind the attractive Modernista mosaic facade of this Barcelona favourite owned by the Escribà family, a name synonymous with sinfully good sweet things.
✉ **La Rambla 83 ☎ 93 301 60 27** Ⓜ **Liceu**
⏰ **8am-9pm**

Formatgeria le Seu
(4, E8) In this old butter-making factory you'll find a scrumptious selection of farmhouse cheeses from all around Spain. The cheeky Scottish woman who owns it speaks reasonably good English and offers 'small plate' tastings on the first Thursday of every month and every Saturday when the neighbourhood sets their stalls out on the street.
✉ **C/de la Dagueria 16, Barri Gòtic ☎ 93 412 65 48** Ⓜ **Jaume I**
⏰ **Mon-Sat 10am-2pm & 5-8pm**

J Murrià (5, G3)
Classic inside and out, this superb traditional-style grocer/delicatessen has been run by the same family since the 1900s and continues to showcase the culinary wonders of Catalunya, Spain and beyond. It's a wonderful place to visit before a picnic or without excuse, and has an eye-catching facade featuring original poster tiles designed by

Escribà

celebrated Modernista painter Ramon Casas.
✉ **C/de Roger de Llúria 85, L'Eixample ☎ 93 215 57 89** Ⓜ **Passeig de Gràcia** ⏰ **Mon-Sat 10am-2pm & 5-8.30pm**

La Pineda (4, D7)
This delightful old-fashioned deli in the heart of Barri Gòtic is sure to bring joy to the hearts of food connoisseurs. It specialises in cured meats, especially *jamon serrano* (cured mountain ham), and a range of cheeses, pâtés and wines, which you can devour and quaff at a little table at the back.
✉ **C/del Pi 16, Barri Gòtic ☎ 93 302 43 93** Ⓜ **Liceu** ⏰ **Mon-Sat 9am-3pm & 5-10pm**

Vila Viniteca (4, F10)
This unassuming little shop has a superb range of Spanish and international wines, from cheap table varieties to vintage treasures, sold by knowledge-able and enthusiastic staff.
✉ **C/dels Agullers 7, La**

Ribera ☎ 93 268 32 27
e www.vilaviniteca.es
Ⓜ Jaume I ⏱ Mon-Sat
9am-2.30pm

Xampany (3, E4)
Put bubbles in your basket
at this atmospheric little
shop lined with hundreds of
varieties and brands of cava,
many of which are stocked
in the original cooler from
the Gran Teatre de Liceu.
✉ C/de València 200,
L'Eixample ☎ 606 33
60 42 Ⓜ Passeig de
Gràcia ⏱ Mon-Sat
10am-2pm & 4.30-9pm
(closed Mon morning
and Sat afternoon)

Window shopping for pure sweet indulgence

FOR CHILDREN

Cuca Fera (4, E10)
Original retro clobber from
the 1960s and '70s for
newborns to eight-year-
olds can be found at this
charismatic new shop near
El Borne.
✉ C/de Cremat Gran 9,
La Ribera ☎ 93 268 37
10 Ⓜ Jaume I ⏱ Mon-
Sat 10am-1.30pm &
4-8pm

Du Pareil au Meme
(5, H1) Fun, durable and
colourful clothes from
Barcelona's only outlet of
this French chain provide
layers for boys and girls
from 3 months to 12 years
old.
✉ Rambla de
Catalunya 95,
L'Eixample ☎ 93 287
14 49 Ⓜ Diagonal
⏱ Mon-Sat 10.30am-
8.30pm

Joguines Foyè (4, E7)
The best toy shop in the
old quarters stocks lots of
traditional playthings such
as tin toys, creepy porcelain

dolls and music boxes as
well as a range of modern
gizmos.
✉ C/dels Banys Nous
13, Barri Gòtic ☎ 93
302 03 89 Ⓜ Liceu
⏱ Mon-Fri 10am-2pm
& 4.30-8pm, Sat 4.30-
8pm

Muller (5, G1)
Exquisite traditional
dresses and suits for newborns to four-year-olds
come from this Catalan
family business, which has
been making clothes in
linen, wool, cotton and silk
to the same designs for the
last 50 years. It specialises
in cherubic christening out-
fits and formal gear.
✉ Rambla de
Catalunya 102,
L'Eixample ☎ 93 488
09 02 Ⓜ Passeig de
Gràcia ⏱ Mon-Sat
10am-2pm &
4.15-8.15pm

Prenatal (3, E6)
Another French chain, this
store has everything you

need for mother and child,
from buggies and cots to
feeding bottles and toys.
Branches at Galeras Maldá
(4, D6; ☎ 93 302 10 95)
and C/de Rosselló (5, F1;
☎ 93 416 07 19).
✉ Gran Vía de les
Corts Catalánes 611,
L'Eixample ☎ 93 302
05 25 e www.prenatal
.es Ⓜ Passeig de
Gràcia ⏱ Mon-Sat
10am-8pm

A melancholy mannequin?

JEWELLERY, PERFUME & ACCESSORIES

Collector's Corner
(6, D5) This cute shop is a veritable Aladdin's cave for fans of fragrance. Along with a dazzling display of ornamental miniatures, you'll find promotion cards, jewellery, powders, beads and everything else that tells some story from the history of perfume. Ask to see the albums of original labels from French companies of the 1920 and '30s which are too precious to display.
✉ Bda de la Llibreteria 8, Barri Gòtic ☎ 93 315 11 05 e www.perfume col.com Ⓜ Jaume I
🕐 Mon-Sat 5-8pm

Forvm Ferlandina
(4, C3) Contemporary jewellery from local designers and European names in everything from plastic to platinum can be found at this shop, which also hosts exhibitions by leading jewellers.
✉ C/de Ferlandina 31, El Raval ☎ 93 441 80 18 e www.forvmjoies .com Ⓜ Universitat
🕐 Mon-Sat 10.30am-2pm & 5-8.30pm

Joaquin Berao
(5, F4) For something very special, head to this elegant store showcasing the exquisite avant-garde creations of one of Spain's most prestigious designers. He works predominantly in silver and gold, and with new and entirely original concepts each season.
✉ C/de Rosselló 277, L'Eixample ☎ 93 218 61 87 e www.joaquin berao.com Ⓜ Diagonal
🕐 Mon-Sat 10.15am-2pm & 5-8.30pm

Loewe (5, J2)
In his guide, *Barcelona*, international art critic Robert Hughes urges anyone with an interest in architecture not to patronise Loewe because of the vandalism they inflicted on this Domènech i Montaner Modernista building. If you're prepared to forgive them – and they have tried to atone for their sin – Loewe is one of the smartest international names in luxurious leather products.
✉ Pg de Gràcia 35, L'Eixample ☎ 93 216 04 00 Ⓜ Passeig de Gràcia 🕐 Mon-Sat 9.30am-8pm

Sephora (4, B5)
This zebra-striped temple of fragrance is the largest in Europe and has every scent you've ever heard of, along with local flavours from Antonio Miró, Jesus Del Pozo, Angel Schlesser and Victorio & Lucchino. A perfume organ allows you to experiment with your perfect eau and, if you don't come up smelling of roses, they'll happily exchange your fragrance.
✉ El Triangle, C/de Pelai 13-39, L'Eixample ☎ 93 306 39 00 e www.sephora.com Ⓜ Catalunya 🕐 Mon-Sat 10am-10pm

Sephora's sensational smell.

Market Squares
Make the most of Barcelona's many markets:
Avda de la Catedral (6, A3) Antiques and bric-a-brac on Thursday
La Rambla (4, H6) Crafts on Saturday and Sunday afternoons
Moll de les Drassanes (4, J6) Antiques and bric-a-brac on weekends
Plaça de Sant Josep Oriol (4, E6) Crafts on Thursday and Friday, art on weekends
Plaça del Pi (4, E6) Artisan food products first Friday and Saturday of the month
Plaça Reial (4, F6) Stamps and coins on Sunday morning

MARKETS

Els Encants Vells

(3, C8) 'The Old Charms' is Barcelona's biggest, best and most authentic flea market where bargain hunters rifle through everything from battered old shoes and assorted junk to antique furniture and new clothes. There are plans to shift the jumble to the outer limits but for now you can find everything here (but also end up losing your wallet if you're not careful) for next to nix – if you *hablo* the lingo.

✉ C/del Dos de Maig (cnr of Plaça de les Glòries), L'Eixample
☎ 93 246 30 30
Ⓜ Glòries ☺ Mon, Wed, Fri & Sat 8.30am-7pm (best choice in mornings)

La Boqueria (4, D5)

One of Europe's best and most famous, this bustling market is laden with atmosphere, colour and all the ingredients that make Spanish cuisine a favourite at the kitchen table. You'll find fresh food of all types here and it's a wonderful place to wander and follow your nose, especially in the morning when it's not full of tourists.

✉ La Rambla 91
☎ 93 318 25 84
Ⓜ Liceu
☺ Mon-Sat 8am-8.30pm

MUSIC

Castelló (4, B5)

This family-run chain of stores has been tickling the earlobes of Catalans since 1935, and comprises six stores in El Raval. Each specialises in a different genre so, between them, you're bound to hit the right chord. There are branches at C/dels Tallers 3 (4, B5), C/dels Tallers 7 (4, B5) and C/dels Tallers 79 (4, A3), as well as at C/Nou de La Rambla 1 (4, F5) and C/de Sant Pau 2 (4, E5).

✉ C/dels Tallers 9, El Raval ☎ 93 412 72 85
ⓔ www.discos castello.es Ⓜ Catalunya
☺ Mon-Sat 10am-2pm & 4.30-8.30pm

CD-Drome (4, B4)

This excellent store has an even range of CDs and vinyl covering the main branches of dance along with the best indie selection in Barcelona.

✉ C/de Valldon Zella 3, El Raval
☎ 93 317 46 46
Ⓜ Universitat
☺ Mon-Sat 10am-2pm & 4-8pm

Etnomusic (4, C5)

From flamenco to samba and whatever jiggles in between, this is your best bet for music from around the globe.

✉ C/Bonsuccés 6, El Raval ☎ 93 301 18 84
ⓔ www.etnomusic.com
Ⓜ Catalunya ☺ Mon 5-8pm, Tues-Sat 11am-2pm & 5-8pm

Eutherpe (4, C4)

Close to the MACBA (p. 34) – although from an entirely different epoch – is this haven for aficionados of medieval and baroque music.

✉ C/d'Elisabets 22, El Raval ☎ 93 412 63 05
Ⓜ Catalunya ☺ Mon-Sat 10.30am-1pm & 4-7pm

La Casa (4, B5)

Some local DJs hate this place so much that you know it's worth a look. Spin for spin, this may be the city's best outlet for dance music and has an impressive range of CDs and vinyl. There are magazines and flyers by the door for local info (if the staff

are too busy). Branch at C/de la Portaferrisa 17 (4, D6; ☎ 93 317 11 80).
✉ Plaça de Vicenç Martorell 4, El Raval
☎ 93 412 33 05
Ⓜ Catalunya ☺ Mon-Sat 11am-2pm & 5-9pm

Verdes Records (4, C7)

This literally underground shop specialises in trip hop but also does a decent line in house and techno. They have sampling decks and plenty of enthusiasm up their sleeve, plus the low-down on other specialist vinyl shops.

✉ C/del Duc de la Victoria 5, Barri Gòtic
☎ 93 301 91 77
Ⓜ Liceu ☺ Mon-Sat 11am-8pm

Wah Wah (4, D3)

Best on a street with lots of decent music shops, Wah Wah is chock-full of 1970s vinyl but also has a good techno section.

✉ C/de la Riera Baixa 14, El Raval ☎ 93 442 37 03 Ⓜ Sant Antoni or Liceu ☺ Mon-Sat 11am-3pm & 5-8.30pm

SPECIALIST STORES

Arlequí Màscares

(4, E9) A little house of horrors (or delights, depending on your mood), this shop specialises in masks to wear and for decoration. Stock also includes a beautiful range of decorative boxes in Catalan themes, and you're welcome to visit the workshop in Poble Espanyol at Balleros 10 (1, A1; ☎ 93 426 21 69).

✉ C/de la Princesa 7, La Ribera ☎ 93 268 27 52 e www.arlequimask .com Ⓜ Jaume I ⏰ Mon-Sat 10.30am-8.30pm, Sun 10.30am-4pm

Casa Morelli (4, E7)

Dealing with the cantankerous old woman who runs this musty old shop is worth it when you see that it's entirely devoted to feathers, all wrapped in tissue and stacked in dusty boxes reaching to the ceiling.

✉ C/dels Banys Nous 15, Barri Gòtic Ⓜ Liceu ⏰ (unreliable) Mon-Fri 5-8pm

Cereria Subirà (6, D5)

Even if you are not interested in candles, you will be impressed by the ornate decor here and can brag about having been to the oldest shop in Barcelona, which starting selling wicks and wax in 1761.

✉ Bda de la Llibreria 7, Barri Gòtic ☎ 93 315 26 06 Ⓜ Jaume I ⏰ Mon-Fri 9am-1.30pm & 4-7.30pm, Sat 9am-1.30pm

Drap (4, D7)

This busy shop brings out the giddy little girl in all of us – which generally comes as a surprise to blokes – as it's packed to the rafters with everything relating to dolls and their wellbeing: everything from miniature jars of jam to intricate handmade mansions.

✉ C/del Pi 14, Barri Gòtic ☎ 93 318 14 87 Ⓜ Mon-Fri 9.30am-1.30pm & 4.30-8.30pm, Sat 10am-5pm

El Ingenio (4, E6)

A bewildering range of tricks, fancy dress, masks and other accessories to liven up your party. Here's where you can get your stick-on Salvador Dalí moustache and go around telling everyone that the moon is made of cheese.

✉ C/d'En Rauric 6, Barri Gòtic ☎ 93 317 71 38 Ⓜ Liceu ⏰ Mon-Sat 10am-2pm & 5-8.30pm

L'Estanc de Laietana

(4, F9) The place where cigar smokers come to feel loved, the entire shop is a humidor and stocks the best cigars from around the world, along with hundreds of brands of cigarettes and rolling tobacco.

✉ Via Laietana 4, La Ribera ☎ 93 310 10 34 e www.geocities .com/estanc Ⓜ Jaume I ⏰ Mon-Fri 9am-2pm & 4-8pm, Sat 10am-2pm

L'Herboristeria del Rei (4, F6)

This soothing shop is framed by a grand balcony and lined with the tiny drawers of herbal specimens that have kept it in business since 1823. The shop took the name when it became court herbalist to Queen Isabel II (but changed it pretty swiftly during the two Republican periods).

✉ C/de Vidre 1, Barri Gòtic ☎ 93 318 05 12 Ⓜ Liceu ⏰ Mon-Sat 10am-2pm & 5-8pm

Norma Comics

(4, A12) The largest comic store in the city has a comic gallery, an astonishing international collection and, next door, an entire shop dedicated to the adventures of Tintin.

✉ Pg de Sant Joan 9, L'Eixample ☎ 93 245 45 26 e www.norma-ed.es Ⓜ Arc de Triomf ⏰ Mon-Sat 10.30am-2pm & 5-8.30pm

Sestienda (4, F6)

Exclusively gay sex shop where you can get your gay map of the city along with all the apparatus required for a happy holiday.

✉ C/d'En Rauric 11 ☎ 93 318 86 76 e www.sestienda.com Ⓜ Liceu ⏰ Mon-Sat 10am-8.30pm

A meaty market stall

places to eat

No matter what your budget or belly size, you'll find something to suit in Barcelona. It teems with cafes and restaurants dishing up everything from tiny tapas to gargantuan feasts. If you're on limited time, the only problem will be deciding what to leave out. Many restaurants specialise in Catalan cooking, whether traditional or experimental, and you'll find a concentration of them in Barri Gòtic and El Raval. Other menus show influence from nearby France while some span the entire Mediterranean seaboard. With the influx of immigrants from other parts of Spain, Barcelona also features diverse regional cuisines from all over the country and these restaurants are spread throughout the city. You'll find as many good seafood restaurants inland as you will by the beach. Ethnic cuisines are becoming increasingly popular and Asian restaurants have been the flavour of recent years.

Meal Costs

The pricing symbols used in this chapter indicate the cost of a two-course meal a la carte, excluding drinks.

$	under €7
$$	€7-15
$$$	€15-25
$$$$	over €25

Martin Hughes

Tapas – the ingenious tradition of combining eating and drinking – is not as big in Barcelona as in other parts of Spain but there's still a variety to choose from. Barcelonins love to eat outdoors and entire blocks are given over to streetside eateries known as *terazzas* (terraces). When al fresco is paramount, just go for a wander until you find your spot. Another fine Catalan institution is the *granja* (dairy bar) where you can indulge in pastries and sweet milky pick-me-ups at any time of the day.

Menu del Dia

Virtually every restaurant in Barcelona has a set lunch menu, consisting of three courses and a drink. They cost about half as much as the same items would from the a la carte menu, and provide the perfect opportunity to sample food from restaurants that might otherwise be out of your price range.

Dining Hours & Booking

Catalans eat late and they eat big: most have three or four courses for lunch (between 2pm and 4pm) while nobody sits down for dinner until at least 9.30pm. Unless you get into sync with the locals you'll find yourself dining exclusively with other blow-ins and usually only in tourist restaurants.

Most places close on Sunday (and holidays), many also keep the shutters down on Monday, lots more close for a few weeks during August and many of the smaller, family-run operations don't like to be tied down by schedules at all.

Because dining out is so popular here, you'd be well advised to reserve a table at mid-range and expensive restaurants during the week and just about everywhere on Friday and Saturday (when many places stay open later).

CATALAN CUISINE

Catalunya has a reputation for producing some of Spain's finest cuisine. And it's not just a matter of a few regional dishes but a gastronomy that is quite distinct from the rest of the country and neighbouring France. As a geographically diverse region, Catalunya produces a variety of fresh, high-quality seafood, meat, poultry, game, fruit and vegetables. These can come in unusual and delicious combinations: meat and seafood (a genre known as *mar i muntanya* – sea and mountain), poultry and fruit, fish and nuts.

The cornerstones of the cuisine are four different **sauces**: *sofregit* (fried onion, tomato and garlic), *samfaina* (similar to ratatouille – sofregit plus red pepper and aubergine or courgette), *allioli* (pounded garlic with olive oil, often with egg yolk added to make it more of a mayonnaise) and *picada* (based on ground almonds and other ingredients, such as garlic, parsley, nuts and breadcrumbs, to suit each dish). These sauces are so ubiquitous that they are rarely mentioned on menus.

Catalans share their love of **rice** with other Spaniards and you'll find local versions of paella and other rice dishes. *Arròs a la cassola* or *arròs a la catalana* is Catalan paella, cooked in an earthenware pot and without saffron, whereas *arròs negre* is rice cooked in cuttlefish ink – much tastier than it might sound. Another speciality is *fideuá*, which is similar to paella but uses vermicelli noodles rather than rice as the base. It is usually served with tomato and meat/sausage or fish. You should also receive a little side dish of allioli to mix in as you wish – if you don't, ask for it.

The Catalan version of the **pizza** is the *coca*. There are many variations, both savoury and sweet, on this theme. The savoury option can come with tomato, onion, pepper and sometimes sardines. The sweet version, often almond-based, is more common and is a standard item at many a *festa* (festival) throughout the year. Look out for it if you've got a sweet tooth. Catalans are passionate about *bolets* (wild mushrooms), often disappearing for days in the autumn to pick them, and *calçots* (large sweet spring onions) that are roasted over live coals, dipped in spicy *romesco* (a finely ground mixture of tomatoes, peppers, onions, garlic, almonds and olive oil) sauce and eaten voraciously when in season from January until May.

Pernil (ham) and *formatge* (cheese) are also culinary constants. The main centres of **cheese** production in Catalunya are in La Seu d'Urgell, the Cerdanya district and the Pallars area in the north-west. Although many traditional cheeses are disappearing, you will still be able to find things such as *formatge de tupí*, a goat's cheese soaked in olive oil, and *gorritxa*, another goat's cheese (made with penicillium mould) that is meltingly soft on the tongue. You'll also find all sorts of **sausages**, using pork meat as a base. Some generic names include *botifarra*, *fuet* (a thin, dried pork sausage) and *longanissa*. The names often seem to apply to very different sausages, depending on where you buy them. Some are spicier than others.

Catalans find it hard to understand why other people put butter on bread when *pa amb tomàquet* – bread sliced and then rubbed with tomato, olive oil, garlic and salt – is so easy and so tasty. **Dessert** is usually a mean *crema Catalana*, the delicious local version of crème brûlée, but you might also be offered *mel i mató*, honey and fresh cream cheese. Another alternative is *music*, dried fruits and nuts, sometimes mixed with ice cream or sweetish cream cheese, and served with a glass of sweet muscatel wine.

LA RAMBLA

The terrace restaurants on La Rambla are all much of an overpriced muchness. While you won't find anywhere particularly good for dinner, all the tables are good for a sip and a snack and provide front row seats for the show.

Café de l'Òpera
(4, E6) $$
Cafe
Opposite the Gran Teatre del Liceu (p. 95), this is the busiest and most atmospheric cafe on an otherwise largely tacky strip. Bohemians and their buddies mingle with tourists beneath the Art Deco opera heroines etched into mirrors. The snacks are so-so and the waiters are marvellously unfussed.
✉ La Rambla 74 ☎ 93 317 75 85 Ⓜ Liceu
🕓 9am-midnight

Café de l'Òpera – diva of La Rambla

Café Zurich (4, B6) $$
Cafe
The original 1920s Café Zurich was one of the city's most famous landmarks and meeting places but it was torn down in 1997 to make way for the department store that now occupies this corner. Its shiny, pseudo-classic replacement may not have the charm but it still has perfectly positioned tables for watching the world go by.
✉ C/de Pelai 39
☎ 93 317 91 53
Ⓜ Catalunya 🕓 Mon-Sat 9am-10pm ♿

Pinotxo (4, D5) $
Market
Immerse yourself in the hurly burly of Boqueria market with a visit to Pinotxo, where the freshest seasonal food in the city is cooked simply and served quickly by a family of characters. That the brother looks a bit like the long-nosed wooden puppet is of no significance because customers named the bar decades ago after the old family dog.
✉ Mercat de la Boqueria, parada 466-470 (just on your right as you enter)
☎ 93 317 17 31
Ⓜ Liceu
🕓 Mon-Sat 6am-5pm ♿

Vegetarian Options
Despite the (un)popular myth, Barcelona needn't mean tortilla tedium for vegetarians. Along with reasonable meat-free restaurants such as **Biocenter** (p. 79), **L'Hortet** (p. 80), **L'Atzavara** (p. 84), and **Comme Bio** (p. 81), you'll find choice and flavour at **Menage a Trois** (p. 77), **Oolong** (p. 78), **La Flauta Mágica** (p. 82), **La Cerería** (p. 76) and **Maoz** (p. 76).

Look for Ⓥ – it indicates that the place concerned is either fully vegetarian or has an excellent selection of vegetarian dishes.

BARRI GÒTIC

Agut (4, G8) **$$**
Catalan
This warm and friendly family-run restaurant appeals to a sedate, mature crowd that digs its traditional and robust Catalan fare. If you order a fillet of beef, that's exactly what you'll get so ask for veggies if you require frills.
✉ C/d'En Gignas 16
☎ 93 315 17 09
Ⓜ Jaume I ⊙ Tues-Sat 1.30-4pm & 9pm-midnight, Sun 1.30-4pm ♿ Ⓥ

Arc Café (4, G8) **$$**
Cafe/Market
Down a quiet medieval lane you'll find this attractive cafe with comfortable cushioned benches and an easy air. It's a great spot to linger over fresh bread and tasty snacks any time of day, and they do a mean huevos fritos con beicon for breakfast – that's ham and eggs to you.
✉ C/d'En Carabassa 19
☎ 93 302 52 04
Ⓜ Drassanes ⊙ Mon-Sat 10am-2am ♿ Ⓥ

Buenas Migas
(6, D4) **$**
Cafe
You'll get reliable and warming comfort food such as pastas and sandwiches in this charming little hole

in the Roman wall. The pared-back decor fits in nicely with the Gothic quarter and the delicious creamy pesto will have you dropping by for more. Branch at Plaça del Bonsuccés 6 (4, C5; ☎ 93 412 16 86).
✉ Bda de Santa Clara 2 (cnr of C/dels Comtes & C/Freneria) ☎ 93 319 13 80 ⓔ www.buenas migas.com Ⓜ Jaume I ⊙ Sun-Thur 9am-9pm, Fri & Sat 9am-10pm Ⓥ

Café d'Estiu – Museu Frederic Mares
(6, C5) **$$**
Cafe
There are splendid views from this beautiful Gothic courtyard under the shadow of the Catedral and the canopy of several citrus trees. Delicious sandwiches and snacks are served throughout the day and there is a wide selection of drinks to wet your whistle. The cafe opens from early April to late October, hence the name estiu (summer).
✉ Plaça Sant Lu 5
☎ 93 310 30 14
Ⓜ Jaume I ⊙ Tues-Sun 10am-10pm Ⓥ

Café Just (4, E9) **$**
Cafe
Run by a foundation that

finds work for people who face discrimination, what this place lacks in ambience it makes up for in kudos. They use non-commercial, usually home-made products and have very cheap deals for breakfast, lunch and snacks (plus a non-smoking area).
✉ C/del Sots-tinent Navarro 18 ☎ 93 310 64 56 Ⓜ Jaume I ⊙ Mon-Fri 8am-6pm ♿ Ⓥ

Can Culleretes
(4, E6) **$$**
Catalan
Barcelona's oldest restaurant (founded in 1786) is still going strong with tourists and locals flocking to enjoy its rambling interior, old-fashioned decor, and enormous helpings of traditional Catalan food. If the wild boar stew doesn't grab you, try the lighter seafood option.
✉ C/de Quintana 5
☎ 93 317 30 22
Ⓜ Liceu ⊙ Tues-Sat 1.30-4pm & 9-11pm, Sun 1.30-4pm (closed for 3 weeks in Jul) ♿

Cometacinc (4, F8) **$$**
Market
If you're searching for eats on a Monday (when many restaurants are closed) look no further than this classy under-stated joint, which serves excellent and modestly priced food fresh from the market. There's a good wine list and, if you're game, take on the 'Fighting Bull Carpaccio' for main.
✉ C/del Cometa 5
☎ 93 310 15 58
Ⓜ Jaume I ⊙ Wed-Mon 8pm-1am ♿ Ⓥ

Start Your Day the Catalan Way

A coffee and pastry is the typical breakfast in Barcelona although the Spanish favourite of churros con chocolate (a deep fried pastry to be dunked in a chocolate drink) is also popular. You can find these at any cafe but if you want something more substantial try **Bar Ra** (p. 79), **Pinotxo** (p. 73), **The Bagel Shop** (p. 79) or **Salero** (p. 82).

El Salón (4, F9) $$$
Catalan/French
Decked out like a 19th-century living room, this colourful and relaxed place is so popular that bookings are near essential. The food is essentially (and sensationally) Catalan, with influences from nearby France, and there is some pretty antique furniture for you to sit on as you inevitably wait for a table.
✉ C/de Hostal d'En Sol 6 ☎ 93 315 21 59 Ⓜ Jaume 1 ⊘ Mon-Sat 1-5pm & 8.30pm-midnight (closed for 2 weeks in Aug)

Els Quatre Gats (4, C7) $$$
Catalan
A former artists' lair where Picasso had his first exhibition, 'the four cats' (Catalan slang for 'a few people') became a legendary base for the Modernisme movement. It now has a smart cafe with reproductions of the original art and decor (and a huge list of beers), as well as an expensive Catalan restaurant out the back.
✉ C/de Montsió 3 bis ☎ 93 302 41 40 Ⓜ Catalunya ⊘ Mon-Sat 9am-2am, Sun 5pm-2am (closed 3 weeks in Aug) ♿ Ⓥ

Granja Dulcinea (4, D6) $
Dairy Bar
Barcelona's most famous, and atmospheric, dairy bar is the perfect place to indulge in sweet, frothy delights such as *suizos* (chocolate with lashings of fresh cream) and to dip *melindros* (soft sugar-coated biscuits) into *cacao-lat* (chocolate) so thick that

you drink it with a spoon, all served by bow-tied waiters.
✉ C/de Petritxol 2 ☎ 93 302 68 24 Ⓜ Liceu ⊘ 9am-1pm & 4.30-8.30pm ♿

Irati (4, E6) $$$
Basque
Catering to committed carnivores, this Basque favourite has tasty tapas at the bar and a fairly formal restaurant out back. The set lunch is much cheaper than the a la carte but try the *porrusalda* (a cold dish of salmon with smoked leek soup) wherever you find it.
✉ C/del Cardenal Casañas 17 ☎ 93 302 30 84 Ⓜ Liceu ⊘ Tues-Sat noon-midnight

Market Cuisine
Many of the restaurants listed here specialise in 'market cuisine', which means that their constantly changing menus are based on whatever looks best at the market each morning rather than a particular style of cooking or category of cuisine.

Juicy Jones (4, E6) $
Vegetarian
The long bar at this bright spot, with its island-hippy paint job, is the perfect place to pep up with any of around 30 healthy juices. But don't bother with the sterile restaurant, which makes you feel like you are paying penance for not eating meat, out the back.
✉ C/del Cardenal Casañas 7 ☎ 93 302 43 30 Ⓜ Liceu ⊘ 1pm-midnight Ⓥ

Jupiter (4, F9) $$
Modern
Lounge on comfy sofas with your favourite people, tuck into innovative delicious salads, *bocadillos* (filled rolls) and pastas,

Bocadillos (filled rolls) for all your lunchtime needs

Guy Moberly

and then peek into the fridge for desserts that are worth a short prison sentence for. But for access to this cool and mellow underground place, you'll have to book (after 4pm).

✉ Jupi 4 ☎ 93 268 36 50 Ⓜ Jaume I ⏱ Tues-Sun 7pm-2am V

La Cerería (4, F7) $
Cafe

Far from the bum-bags and camcorders, yet in the heart of Barri Gòtic, this cooperative is a terrific place to chill out, surrounded by young Barcelonins filling the colourful room with smoke and bonhomie. On offer are tasty (mainly) vegetarian dishes such as *bocadillos* (filled rolls), home-made desserts, fruit shakes and fragrant teas.

✉ Bda de Sant Miquel 3-5, just off Plaça de Sant Miquel ☎ 93 301 85 10 Ⓜ Liceu ⏱ Mon-Sat 9.30am-10pm V

La Pla (4, F8) $$$
Mediterranean

The most chic choice in the Gothic quarter, this place has black-and-white menus featuring photographs of staff in action, mainly serving superb and innovative modern Mediterranean dishes with Asian twists and making guests feel warmly welcome.

✉ C/de Bellafila 5 ☎ 93 412 65 52 Ⓜ Jaume I ⏱ 9pm-midnight (until 1am Fri & Sat) ♿ V

La Verónica (4, F7) $$
Pizzeria

The weekday set lunch at this shiny pizza joint is fantastic value with generous salads, feisty pizzas, average desserts and belated coffees. The *porros* (Gorgonzola, leek, mozzarella and tomato) pizza is a standout, and the service slow, sassy and forgivable.

✉ C/d'Avinyó 30 ☎ 93 412 11 22 Ⓜ Liceu ⏱ Tues 8pm-1.30am, Wed-Sun noon-1.30am V ♿ fair

L'Antic Bocoi del Gótic (4, F8) $$
Catalan

Fans of cheese on toast will go weak at the knees when they approach this smart restaurant, from where the smell of the house speciality, *coques gratinadas* (a version of a pizza with Catalan bread) wafts throughout the neighbourhood. There are dozens of mouth-watering varieties to try.

✉ Bda de Viladecois 3 ☎ 93 310 50 67 Ⓜ Jaume I ⏱ 8.30pm-midnight V ♿ good

Los Caracoles (4, G6) $$$$
Catalan

This 19th-century tavern is Barri Gòtic's most picturesque restaurant and is famous for its spit-roast chickens. These days it's frequented by tourists rather than the celebrities whose photos adorn its walls but they still serve the same robust Catalan food that drew the likes of John Wayne here in the first place.

✉ Ptge dels Escudellers 14 ☎ 93 302 31 85 Ⓜ Drassanes ⏱ 1pm-midnight ♿

Maoz (4, F6) $
Middle Eastern

This vegan-friendly Israeli shop serves the best falafel we've ever tasted, and

---

Eating with Children

Kids are welcome at most restaurants although it's rare to find special menus, portions and high chairs. Look for the ♿ icon listed with individual reviews for more kid-friendly options.

Take a long, leisurely lunch at La Verónica.

Martin Hughes

judging from the constant queues of students, travellers, blue-collar workers and beggars, we're not alone. With some judicious stacking from the salad bar, your little snack could last you the day.

✉ C/de Ferran 13
Ⓜ Liceu ⏱ noon-10pm ⚹ Ⓥ

Margarita Blue
(4, H7) $$
Mexican

This lively, loud and hip spot is full every night with lithe young lookers checking themselves out in the assortment of old mirrors behind the bar. The Mexican food is surprisingly creative, satisfying and obviously not unkind on the hips. The same folks run the cruisier **Rita Blue** at Plaça Sant Agustí (4, E5; ☎ 93 412 34 38), which serves up Mediterranean fare.

✉ Josep Anselm Clavé 6, ☎ 93 317 71 76
Ⓜ Drassanes ⏱ 1.30-4pm & 8pm-1.30am

Mastroque (4, G7) $$$
Spanish/French

This former dairy factory has high ceilings, grand arches and rustic chic through and through. If you're tired of trying to decipher menus, just tell Jean Francois what you feel like and he'll deliver a cavalcade of Spanish and French flavours that are guaranteed to make your palate spin.

✉ C/del Còdols 29
☎ 93 301 79 24
Ⓜ Drassanes ⏱ Tues-Fri 1.30-3.30pm & 9-11.30pm, Sat 9-11.30pm, Mon 1.30-3.30pm ⚹ Ⓥ

Martin Hughes

Los Caracoles (p. 76)

Menage a Trois
(4, C6) $$
Market

This gay and groovy new place is one of the city's best and provides an unceasingly cool terrace for summer chillin'. Adventurous cooking puts creative twists on classic themes without pretension and there's a new vegetarian daily special. Don't miss the *Crema Menage a Trois* dessert, which you'll probably want to take home.

✉ C/del Bot 4
☎ 93 301 55 42
Ⓜ Catalunya ⏱ Mon-Sat 9am-11pm Ⓥ

Mesón del Café
(6, E4) $
Cafe

Cramped or cosy depending on your mood, this charming cafe is the ideal spot to while away a rainy afternoon or take the weight off

With a View to...

There is one table upstairs at the bar **La Vinya del Senyor** (p. 89) where you can look at Barcelona's most impressive church and across one of its loveliest plaças, while sipping cava and munching delicious morsels. **Café d'Estiu** (p. 74) has a delightful atmosphere and views from within the heart of Barri Gòtic, while **Mirablau** (p. 90) has the most impressive panorama of the city. **Ruccola** (p. 86) offers a splendid vista over the Med, while the grounds of the Castell de Montjuïc (1, A5) is the place for a picnic with fresh air and a breathtaking view of the city. Otherwise, find your favourite square and there'll surely be a pavement table to view it from.

Looking for Paella?

To save you scanning these pages looking for this Spanish speciality, you could try **7 Portes** (p. 86), **Restaurant Pitarra** (below) or **Senyor Parellada** (p. 83), all of which are renowned for the rice dish named after the two-handled pan in which it served.

One of Spain's biggest exports: paella

Oliver Strewe

any old time. Your entertaining host likes nothing more than engaging in some friendly pidgin banter with the passing trade.
✉ C/la Llibreteria 16
☎ 93 315 07 54
Ⓜ Jaume I ⏱ Mon-Sat 7.30-10.30pm ⚹

Oolong (4, F8) $$
Modern

That they have wind chimes for their service bell and a dog hatch in the kitchen door is an indication of the mood in this cool and cosy restaurant. Add predominantly veggie cooking and you've got one of the best restaurants in the city.
✉ C/d'En Gignás 25
☎ 93 315 12 59
Ⓜ Jaume I ⏱ Mon-Sat 8pm-1am, Sun 8pm-midnight (closed first 3 weeks in Sept)
⚹ Ⓥ ♿ fair

Polenta (4, G9) $$
Modern

So new they hadn't even erected a sign at the time of writing, this place was already packing in the punters just by word of mouth. Expect healthy and very tasty fare based on Mediterranean produce and Asian techniques. For dessert, try the aphrodisiac Charlotte (vanilla, warm chocolate and ginger).
✉ C/Ample 51 ☎ 93 268 14 29 Ⓜ Jaume I
⏱ Mon & Wed-Sun 1pm-midnight Ⓥ

Restaurant Pitarra (4, G8) $$$$
Catalan

This restaurant, established in 1890, occupies the house where the 19th-century playwright Serafi Pitarra penned most of his work. The walls are crammed with old art and the food is

traditional Catalan. If the splayed pig with half his hindquarters carved off doesn't grab you, the Valentian paella surely will.
✉ C/d'Avinyó 56
☎ 93 301 16 47
Ⓜ Drassanes ⏱ Mon-Sat 1-4pm & 8-11pm
⚹ ♿ fair

Schilling (4, E6) $
Cafe

Far away from the relentless rhythm of the street, this elegant and dimly-lit cafe echoes the grand coffee parlours of yesteryear. It has a range of very respectable *bocadillos* (filled rolls) and desserts, light and heavy refreshments, and is a favourite pit stop for stylish gay men. It's not exclusive although the service frequently is.
✉ C/de Ferran 23
☎ 93 317 67 87
Ⓜ Liceu
⏱ 9am-midnight

Self-Naturista (4, B6) $
Vegetarian

This sterile, self-service vegetarian place is like a school canteen, only the chips and peas are replaced by fruit, salads, stews and pasta. Expect to queue for the excellent four-course set lunch. Outside the main feeding hours the dishes are cold and the juices flat but it's still good for a no-frills culinary pit-stop.
✉ C/de Santa Anna 13
☎ 93 318 26 84
Ⓜ Catalunya ⏱ Mon-Sat 11.30am-10pm Ⓥ

Slokai (4, F8) $$$
Market

These young upstarts thumb their nose at

culinary convention and thrill a young and fashionable crowd with menus combining innovation and seasonal availability. You're probably paying a little extra for the perception of cool but a top meal is guaranteed and weekend DJs will get you primed for a night on the tiles.
✉ C/del Palau 5
☎ 93 301 79 42
Ⓜ Jaume I ⏲ Mon-Fri 1.30-3.30pm & 9.30pm-midnight, Sat 9.30pm-midnight ♨ **V** ♿ fair

Taxidermista
(4, F6)   **SSS**
Mediterranean
These days it's mainly tourists getting stuffed in this old taxidermist shop, once patronised by Salvador Dalí. In summer, the terrace is a great spot to look out over the shenanigans of Plaça Reial while tucking into solid Catalan and Mediterranean fare.
✉ Plaça Reial 8 ☎ 93 412 45 36 Ⓜ Liceu
⏲ restaurant 1.30-4pm & 8.30-11.30pm; bar & tapas Tues-Sun 1.30pm-1am **V**

> ### Deals & Dinners
> If you're in town for business, **Brasserie Flo** (p. 81) and **Senyor Parellada** (p. 83) are sober and satisfying, **Cal Pep** (p. 81) is a less formal choice and **East 47** (p. 84) is the place to make an impression.

The Bagel Shop
(4, C6)   **S**
Cafe
When you need a break from rich Catalan food, this bright and chirpy neighbourhood joint does tasty and innovative bagels and toppings, as well as soups, salads and sweets. It's also handy for a picnic shop and you can buy your doughy rings by the armful.
✉ C/de la Canuda 25
☎ 93 302 41 61
Ⓜ Catalunya ⏲ Mon-Sat 11am-4pm ♨ **V**

Tostaderos Bon Mercat (6, D5)   **SS**
Cafe
Discerning coffee drinkers should make a beeline for this little place, which serves the best beans in town. The smell and taste of their gourmet coffees

will make your head spin and your palate dance.
✉ Bda de la Llibreteria 1-3 ☎ 93 202 14 80
Ⓜ Jaume I ⏲ Mon-Sat 8am-8pm ♨

Venus Delicatessen
(4, F7)   **SS**
Cafe
This is where the locals come for casual tête-à-têtes, and a glowing love heart lampshade throws a soft light over cute marble-top tables for two. The deli-style dishes are scrawny by Spanish standards but it's important to keep some room for the home-made desserts and not be too bloated to flirt with the staff.
✉ C/d'Avinyó 25
☎ 93 301 15 85
Ⓜ Jaume I ⏲ Mon-Sat noon-midnight **V**

EL RAVAL

Bar Kasparo (4, B5) **SS**
Market
There's atmospheric terrace dining beneath arches at this friendly place, which takes over an entire corner of a plaça dominated by a relatively calm children's playground. It's run by three friendly Australian sisters and does a sturdy line in tapas, mixed salads, filled rolls and hot dishes that change daily.
✉ Plaça de Vicenç Martorell 4 ☎ 93 302

20 72 Ⓜ Catalunya ⏲ 9am-midnight (closed Christmas to Feb) ♨ **V**

Bar Ra (4, D5)   **SS**
Modern
This cool hangout is the best reason to venture into the forbidding car park behind Boqueria market and illuminates El Raval with a groovy twinkle. There's terrace dining in summer and along a sheltered and atmospheric

alleyway in winter. The 'exotic' menu occasionally misses the mark but the portions are huge, the music invigorating and the waiters exceedingly cute.
✉ Plaça de la Gardunya 3 ☎ 93 423 18 78 Ⓜ Liceu ⏲ Mon-Sat 9am-2am **V**

Biocenter (4, C4)   **SS**
Vegetarian
You share your table with whoever at this large and friendly veggie restaurant,

Coffee Primer & Tea Warning

Coffee comes in three categories and two languages. Here we use Catalan: *café con leche* (drunk at breakfast) is coffee with milk, *café solo* is an espresso and a *café cortado* is an espresso cut with a splash of milk. A *carajillo* is a café solo with a shot of brandy, a very effective eye-opener. Barcelonins don't drink much tea and it's usually black when they do. Request milk separately *(a parte)* and avoid asking for tea in a place where it's not usually served – you'll probably regret it.

Martin Hughes

which serves an extensive assortment of salads, casseroles and seasonal vegetables cooked using various techniques from around the world. There's also a front room where you can get stuck into organic beer and a natural health-food shop across the road.

✉ **C/del Pintor Fortuny 25** ☎ **93 301 45 83**
Ⓜ **Liceu** ◷ **Mon-Sat 1pm-midnight**
♿ **V** & **good**

El Caféti (4, E4) **$$**
Catalan/French
Down a busy alleyway, far away from passing tourist trade, you'll find this faded old world charm that feels like a familiar, well thumbed paperback. Its menu of Catalan favourites such as *bacalao* (salted cod) hasn't changed much in nearly 20 years.

✉ **C/de l'Hospital 99**
☎ **93 329 24 19**
Ⓜ **Liceu** ◷ **Tues-Sat 1.30-3.30pm & 9-11.30pm, Sun 1.30-3.30pm** ♿

Estevet 15 (4, B3) **$$**
Catalan
There's nourishment for soul *and* body at this

wonderfully atmospheric old restaurant, where generations of the Suñé family – whose warm and hearty hospitality is unrivalled – have been enticing customers with their robust brand of Catalan fare for more than a century. Footballers Diego Maradona and Gary Lineker were regulars when they played at Barça.

✉ **C/de Valldon Zella 46** ☎ **93 302 41 86**
Ⓜ **Universitat**
◷ **Mon-Sat 1.30-4pm & 9-11pm** ♿

Granja Viader
(4, C5) **$**
Cafe
The fifth generation of the same family runs this atmospheric milk bar and cafe, which was set up in 1873 as the first to bring farm freshness to the city. They invented *cacaolat*, the chocolate and skimmed milk drink now popular all over Spain, and continue to be innovative purveyors of all things milky.

✉ **C/d'En Xuclá 4-6**
☎ **93 318 34 86**
Ⓜ **Liceu** ◷ **Mon 5-9pm, Tues-Sat 9am-1.45pm & 5-9pm** ♿ **V**

L'Hortet (4, C4) **$$**
Vegetarian
It won't be the kooky op shop art of overdressed women that strikes you when you enter this cosy family-run place, it's the novelty of being able to smell the cooking in the smoke (and booze) free environment. Set menus change nightly but are always reliable for simple, wholesome fare from dhal to enchiladas.

✉ **C/del Pintor Fortuny 32** ☎ **93 317 61 89**
Ⓜ **Liceu** ◷ **1-4pm daily plus Thur-Sun 8.30-11.30pm** ♿ **V** & **fair**

Mama Café
(4, C4) **$$$**
Modern
A cosy cross between colourful country house and stark urban warehouse, this place is sassy, sexy and stylish. The market fresh Mediterranean cuisine is big on taste but *nouvelle* in quantity, the soundtrack is in the vicinity of Acid Jazz and the house wine is best avoided.

✉ **C/del Doctor Dou 10**
☎ **93 301 29 40**
Ⓜ **Catalunya** ◷ **Mon 1-4pm, Tues-Sat 1-4pm & 9pm-midnight**
♿ **V** & **good**

Muebles Navarro
(4, D3) **$$**
Cafe
This used to be a furniture shop and maintains the look with an amalgam of different recycled tables and chairs stretching out over three long and elegant rooms. Perfect for a group chat and snack, day or night, with remarkably good sandwiches and desserts, including a jolly good

cheesecake.

✉ C/de la Riera Alta 4-6 ☎ 607 18 80 96 Ⓜ San Antonio ◔ Sun & Mon 6pm-12.30am, Fri & Sat 6pm-3am ⅋ good

Salsitas (4, G5) **$$$**
Mediterranean
This palace of whiteness has sculpted palm trees and colourful projections, and is full of dolled-up tourists and glam locals. Mediterranean dishes with a splash

of Oriental are tasty but small and overpriced. After midnight, it becomes the ultra-trendy Club 22 where everyone's a sweetie and cocktails are *de rigueur*.

✉ C/Nou de la Rambla 22 ☎ 93 318 08 40 Ⓜ Liceu ◔ restaurant 8pm-midnight daily, club Wed-Sat midnight-4am ⅋ V ⅋ excellent

Silenus (4, C4) **$$$**
Modern
Mucho chic, this is one of

the most elegant establishments in El Raval, serving dishes as colourful, sumptuous and refined as the decor. Even if you're not hungry, make sure you pop in for a drink just to appreciate the atmosphere.

✉ C/dels Àngels 8 ☎ 93 302 26 80 Ⓜ Universitat ◔ restaurant Mon 2-4pm, Tues-Sat 1-4pm & 9-11.30pm; bar Tues-Sat 10am-1am

LA RIBERA

Brasserie Flo
(4, A8) **$$$**
Brasserie
This immense, discreet brasserie is the perfect setting for a high-powered lunch. The decor is a sober blend of Modernista and modern, the food representative of the best of Catalunya and France and the desserts, if not to die for, are at least worthy of great pain.

✉ C/de les Jonqueres 10 ☎ 93 319 31 02 Ⓜ Urquinaona ◔ 1-4pm & 8.30pm-1am ⅋ ⅋ good

Café Kafka
(4, E11) **$$$**
Modern
This artsy restaurant and hangout has a very cool metallic and tan interior, and a high ceiling illuminated by giant tea candles. The sound system is equally crisp, tending to mellow jazz, and the menu is a wonderful concoction of Mediterranean staples with elaborate Oriental and Arabian flourishes. Service is friendly and without any

airs or graces.

✉ C/de la Fusina 7 ☎ 93 310 85 26 Ⓜ Arc de Triomf ◔ restaurant Sun-Thur 9pm-midnight, Fri & Sat 9pm-1am; bar Sun-Thur 9pm-1am, Fri & Sat 9pm-3am

Cal Pep (4, F11) **$$$**
Tapas
This boisterous tapas bar brims with energy and personality, thanks largely to Pep, the owner and chef, who keeps his customers amused with a constant stream of banter while he grills the sensational seafood tapas for which this restaurant is famous. He also runs the more expensive **Passadis del Pep** at Plaça del Palau 2 (4, F11; ☎ 93 310 10 21).

✉ Plaça de les Olles 8 ☎ 93 310 79 61 Ⓜ Barceloneta ◔ Mon 8-11.45pm, Tues-Sat 1.15-4pm & 8-11.45pm

Comme Bio (4, D9) **$$**
Vegetarian
Where vegetarianism is a

celebration rather than a chore, large and stylish Comme Bio has an enormous range of additive and chemical-free dishes, from creative tapas to sturdy mains. There are vegan dishes, organic drinks, English menus on request and a wholefood shop full of artisanal products. Branch at Gran Vía de les Corts Catalánes 603 (5, K2; ☎ 93 301 03 76).

✉ Via Laietana 28 ☎ 93 319 89 68 Ⓜ Jaume I ◔ 1-4pm & 8.30-11.30pm V

Commerç 24
(4, D11) **$$**
Modern
The hippest restaurant in town (until the next hippest restaurant comes along), this place has a modern menu traversing the globe with flavours pulled in from all four corners. It is at its most lively in the grey monochrome and citrus minimalism at the front.

✉ C/del Comerç 24 ☎ 93 319 21 02 Ⓜ Arc de Triomf ◔ Tues-Sat 1.30-4pm & 7.30-11pm

De Va Vi (4, E10) $$$
Wine Bar
It was recently discovered that this building used to house Christopher Columbus when he was in town. It's now a beautifully sedate wine bar, where you can enjoy the best local cheeses and wine beneath huge Gothic arches and other enchanting original 15th-century features.
✉ C/de Banys Vells 16
☎ 93 319 29 00
Ⓜ Jaume I
🕓 7pm-midnight

Estrella de Plata (4, F11) $$$
Tapas
Top for tapas that you won't find anywhere else, this shi-shi bar combines elegant table settings, white-clad waiting staff and exquisitely presented 'designer' tapas. Beautiful black-and-white photographs on the walls contrast nicely with the decor and offer an evocative tour of Barcelona's history.
✉ Plaça de Palau
☎ 93 268 06 35
Ⓜ Barceloneta
🕓 Mon-Sat 1.30-4pm & 8pm-midnight ♿ good

Idea (4, E11) $
Internet Cafe
For somewhere more engaging than a place to check your email, pop into this thinking den that combines cyber technology with the atmosphere of a traditional library. While thumbing through the international papers, you can fuel up on tapas, snacks and teasing cakes.
✉ Plaça Comercial
☎ 93 268 87 87
Ⓜ Jaume I 🕓 8am-1am (until 3am Fri & Sat, until 11pm Sun) Ⓥ

La Flauta Mágica (4, E10) $$$
Vegetarian
It seems like everything here, from the decor to the music, is deliberately understated to let the flavour and presentation of the food stand out even more. Dishes – mainly vegetarian with a few organic meat items – are small but very tasty and, while there are few Johnny Foreigners around, they do have an English menu.
✉ Banys Vells 18
☎ 93 268 46 94
Ⓜ Jaume I 🕓 1.30pm-midnight ♿ Ⓥ

La Tinaja (4, F11) $$
Spanish
To indulge in the Spanish passions of *jamón* (ham), cheese, pâtés and wine, head to this candle-lit and ambient place, housed on the ground floor of a 17th-century palace. The walls are lined with shelves of *tinajas* (urns) and the room is filled with soft classical Spanish guitar and chatter.
✉ C/de l'Espartería 9
☎ 93 310 22 50
Ⓜ Barceloneta
🕓 Mon-Sat 6pm-2am Ⓥ

Little Italy (4, E11) $$$
Italian
Well known for its jazz sessions on Wednesday and Thursday nights, this place has a stylish mix of Mediterranean dishes, some of them loosely Italian. It's decorated in the style of New York's Italian quarter in SoHo and attracts a varied crowd.
✉ C/del Rec 30
☎ 93 319 79 73
Ⓜ Barceloneta
🕓 Mon-Sat 1.30-4pm & 9pm-midnight (closed 2 weeks in Aug)

Pla de la Garsa (4, D10) $$
Catalan
This staunchly Catalan restaurant was Barcelona's hippest hangout during the twilight of Franco's reign. Scattered with antiques and original 19th-century fixtures, today it's still the most enchanting. The whole Catalan caboodle is good but the highlights are the superb wines, cheeses and desserts. The quaint pop-up menus come in several languages but 'never' Castilian.
✉ C/dels Assaonadors 13 ☎ 93 315 24 13
Ⓜ Jaume I 🕓 Tues-Sun 8pm-1am ♿

Sagardi (4, F10) $$
Basque/Tapas
Pause at this popular local bar and you'll inevitably see tourists stuffing their faces (and occasionally bags) with delicious Basque tapas, which they somehow presume to be free. How long Sagardi will continue to rely on the honesty system, of cocktail sticks used, is anyone's guess.
✉ C/de l'Argentería 64
☎ 93 319 99 93
Ⓜ Jaume I
🕓 noon-midnight

Salero (4, E11) $$$
Mediterranean/Cafe
This cool white refuge, in the fashionable El Borne, is the embodiment of understated cool and is an ideal place to relax after, or during, a day of holiday bustle. The food is magnificently Mediterranean with Asian flirtations, and gourmet breakfasts include the likes of sinfully good brie jaffles.
✉ C/del Rec 60
☎ 93 319 80 22
Ⓜ Barceloneta

⊙ Mon-Thur 9am-4pm & 9pm-2am, Fri 9am-4pm & 9pm-3am, Sat 8pm-3am **V** & good

Sandwich & Friends
(4, E11)   **$$**
Cafe
On busy nights – most nights – you can hardly move in this fashionable hangout without tripping over a scooter helmet. All the dishes are named after friends of the owners, a popular bunch judging by the 70 or so salads and *bocadillos* (filled rolls) on offer. The huge Pop Art frescoes splashed along the walls are from the hand of Jordi Labanda.
⊠ Pg del Born 27
☎ 93 310 07 86
Ⓜ Jaume I
⊙ 1pm-1am **V**

Santa Maria Tapas
(4, D11)   **$$$**
Tapas
Swing through the doors of this snazzy place for what many regard as the best tapas in town. Beautifully decked out and always busy, its innovative and specialist tapas range from falafel to sushi as well as lots of new spins on Spanish favourites (black sausage with anise and orange anyone?), all prepared with zest.
⊠ C/del Commerç 55
☎ 93 315 12 27 Ⓜ Arc de Triomf ⊙ Tues-Sat 1.30-3.30pm & 8.30pm-12.30am **V**

Senyor Parellada
(4, E9)   **$$$**
Catalan/French
In the smart, lemon dining room of this attractive 18th-century building, you'll find old-fashioned Catalan recipes such as *escalivada* (grilled peppers, aubergine and onions) prepared with contemporary panache. Some dishes come in half portions, handy for sampling, but be prepared to queue for lunch or book for dinner.
⊠ C/de l'Argenteria 37
☎ 93 310 50 94
Ⓜ Jaume I ⊙ Mon-Sat 1-3.30pm & 8.30-11.30pm ♣ & good

The Tèxtil Café
(4, E10)   **$**
Cafe
This soothing cafe is set in a beautifully tranquil 15th-century courtyard. That it gets as many locals as tourists is a measure of its appeal. Terrific snacks such as toasted sandwiches, salads and different hot dishes are available daily, as well as a huge range of booze.
⊠ C/de Montcada 12-14 ☎ 93 268 25 98
Ⓜ Jaume I ⊙ Tues-Thur 10am-midnight, Fri & Sat 10am-3am, Sun 6-10pm ♣ **V**

Vasculum Bar & Tapas (4, F10)   **$$**
Tapas
An extensive menu comprising Catalan tapas with influences from wherever they please. Assorted Iberian cold cuts for €12 is a good snack for two before heading to El Borne for a night on the razzle. The restaurant is unremarkable but the terrace, in front of the church, is special.
⊠ Plaça de Santa Maria del Mar ☎ 93 319 01 67 Ⓜ Jaume I ⊙ restaurant 1.30-4pm & 8.30pm-midnight, tapas Mon-Thur 10.30am-midnight, Fri & Sat 10.30pm-1.30am **V**

Xampanyet (4, F10) **$$**
Tapas
As you emerge from the museums on this street you might be snared by the smell of anchovies wafting out of this colourful and charming seafood tapas bar. Its specialities are seafood titbits, cava and champagne, and the room is lined with cute blue tiles and has barrels of bonhomie.
⊠ C/de Montcada 22
☎ 93 319 70 03
Ⓜ Jaume I
⊙ Sun noon-4pm, Tues-Sat noon-4pm & 6.30-11pm ♣

Start the day as you mean to go on.

Martin Hughes

L'EIXAMPLE

Casa Calvet
(5, K4) $$$$
Mediterranean
Set on the ground floor of a Gaudí apartment block, this sophisticated restaurant is patronised by the most important people in Spain, who come here for creative Mediterranean cooking with a Catalan bent. Even if you don't enjoy your foie gras or ravioli stuffed with oysters, you can still savour Gaudí's genius.
✉ C/de Casp 48
☎ 93 412 40 12
Ⓜ Urquinaona
⏰ Mon-Sat 1-3.30pm & 9-11pm ♣ ♿ good

Ciudad Condal
(3, F5) $$
Tapas
Join the smart l'Eixample set and choose from up to 50 different tapas including salads and *flautas* (tapas served on baguettes), which are more expensive – but larger – than in other tapas joints. It's cheaper if you eat at the bar, cooler on the terrace and more formal in the restaurant.
✉ Rambla de Catalunya 18 ☎ 93 18 19 97 Ⓜ Passeig de Gràcia ⏰ Mon-Sat 7am-1.30am, Sun 8am-1.30am ♿ fair

East 47 (5, G3) $$$$
Mediterranean
Named after Andy Warhol's New York studio factory, and featuring some of his original Pop Art, this is where Barcelona's most beautiful people come to chow. You can pop in for a cocktail, some beluga caviar on toast or a full Mediterranean banquet that will make your head spin and your wallet sag.
✉ C/de Pau Claris 150
☎ 93 487 46 47
Ⓜ Passeig de Gràcia
⏰ food Mon-Sat 1-4pm & 8pm-1am; cocktails 11am-1.30am daily

El Asador de Burgos
(5, G4) $$$$
Spanish
Committed carnivores will love this 'roasting house', where joints are cooked slowly in traditional ovens and what you see is what you get. Suckling pig with crispy crackling is the speciality. Advance booking is essential.
✉ C/del Bruc 118
☎ 93 207 31 60
Ⓜ Verdaguer ⏰ Mon-Sat 1-4pm & 8.30-11.30pm ♣ ♿ fair

L'Atzavara (3, E4) $
Vegetarian
Outrageously good value (which is why there are usually queues out front) this place is nothing special to look at but the grub is good. The three-course lunch changes daily but always includes salads and international vegetarian favourites such as macaroni and lasagne.
✉ C/de Muntaner 109
☎ 93 454 59 25
Ⓜ Universitat ⏰ Mon-Sat 1-4pm ♣ Ⓥ

Mauri Patisserie
(5, G1) $$
Cafe
Join the ladies who lunch for exquisite pastries, light snacks and piped music. The plush interior is capped by an ornately painted ceiling at the entrance, which dates back to Mauri's first days in 1929. This is the kind of place that your mum would love.
✉ Rambla de Catalunya 103
☎ 93 215 81 46
Ⓜ Diagonal
⏰ 9am-9pm ♣ Ⓥ

Wines
Although not as much as some of their fellow countrymen, Barcelonins drink a lot of wine and it accompanies most meals. The three varieties are *blanco* (white), *tinto* (red) and *rosado* (rosé). Unless you go to an old-fashioned *bodega* (wine bar) or a restaurant that specialises in wine, don't expect much from the house varieties. The Penedès (p. 55), just over half an hour south-west of Barcelona, is one of the best wine-growing regions in Spain. The whites are better than the red but the area is best known for the Spanish bubbly, *cava*.

Semproniana
(3, E3)　　　　　$$$
Catalan
This place is gorgeously decorated with works from local artists. The chef owner is a member of the Parellada restaurant dynasty and she cooks up a veritable storm of modern Catalan dishes, which are so popular that booking is highly recommended.
✉ C/del Rosselló 148

☎ 93 453 18 20
Ⓜ Hospital Clinic
◷ Mon-Sat 1.30-4pm & 9-11.30pm ♿

Tragaluz
(5, G1)　　　　　$$$$
Mediterranean
This restaurant for the well heeled is named after the spectacular skylight that crowns the dining room. The food is fab, drawing inspiration from all over

the Mediterranean, and there's an equally cool cocktail lounge downstairs. The same people run the pricey Japanese restaurant, **El Japonés**, just across the road.
✉ Ptge de la Concepció 5
☎ 93 487 01 96
Ⓜ Diagonal
◷ Mon-Sun 1.30-4pm & Wed-Sat 8pm-midnight V

GRÀCIA

Botafumeiro
(5, C1)　　　　　$$$$
Galician/Seafood
The seafood in this Galician treasure is about as fresh as you'll get without getting wet. Lobster, scallops, oysters and other shellfish are kept in a Jacuzzi at the door, waiting to be served at business dinners and family occasions in the bustling restaurant. Guitar players and singers contribute to the cheerful clamour.
✉ Gran de Gràcia 81
☎ 93 218 42 30
Ⓜ Fontana ◷ Mon-Sat 1pm-1am ♿ V ♿ fair

Flash Flash (3, D3)　$$
Modern
Barcelona's first ever designer bar is the height of 1960s cool with long, luxurious leather banquettes and white walls adorned with pictures of a Twiggy-esque photographer prancing about taking snaps. The menu consists of hundreds of different omelettes, including some for dessert, and a 'girl's' one that comes with bechamel sauce. It gets quite a mixed and conservative crowd.
✉ Granada del

Penedès ☎ 93 237 09 90 ⓡ FCG Gràcia
◷ 1pm-1am
♿ V ♿ fair

Jean-Luc Figueras
(5, E2)　　　　　$$$$
Catalan/French
One of the jewels in the crown of Barcelona's culinary scene, everything about this restaurant – right down to the crayon-drawn individual menus – has the mark of head chef and renowned local foodie, Jean-Luc Figueras. The food, Catalan with French flair, is exceptional, the service impeccable, the decor elegantly understated and the art adorning the walls – in our opinion – rubbish.
✉ C/Santa Teresa 10
☎ 93 415 28 77
Ⓜ Diagonal ◷ Mon-Fri 1.30-3.30pm & 8.30-11pm, Sat 8.30-11pm ♿ V ♿ good

La Gavina (5, C1)　$$
Italian
Like the seagull in the name, we'll stick our necks out and say these are the best pizzas in Barcelona. Thin-crust, innovative and

seasonal, every single one is a winner although the Catalana (topped with seasonal mushrooms) takes home the rosette. Make a good impression and you might find yourself with a complimentary *mariconada* (little gay thing) with Tia Maria, coffee and cream.
✉ C/Ros de Olano 19 (no sign but it's opposite Antoni Llobet's hairdressers)
Ⓜ Fontana ◷ Tues-Sun 8pm-1am V

La Singular (5, D2)　$$
Mediterranean/Market
The menu at this hip, cosy and Lesbian-run restaurant depends on what caught the chef's eye at the market that day. It's obvious that the creative cooks get as much of a kick out of seasonal produce as the folks of Gràcia who make bookings near-essential here.
✉ C/Francisco Giner 50
☎ 93 237 50 98
Ⓜ Diagonal
◷ Mon-Fri 1-4pm & 8pm-midnight, Sat 1-4pm & 8pm-1am
V ♿ good

L'Illa de Gràcia
(5, D1) **$**
Vegetarian
Every expense is spared on the decor here but, at long last, this is a vegetarian restaurant where you can drink and smoke. Expect cannelloni, crepes, salads, lasagne and the like but the food is cheap because they skimp on flavour.
✉ C/de Sant Doménec 19 ☎ 93 238 02 29
Ⓜ Fontana ⏲ Tues-Fri 1-4pm & 9pm-midnight, Sat & Sun 2-4pm & 9pm-midnight ⚥ Ⓥ

Sol Soler (5, C2) **$$**
Tapas
On a corner of Gràcia's most lively plaça, this busy wholefood tapas bar has faded bohemian chic, relaxed music, intimate lighting and marble tables on which to enjoy a range of tasty and predominantly vegetarian fare.
✉ Plaça del Sol 21-22
☎ 93 217 44 40
Ⓜ Fontana ⏲ Mon & Tues 7pm-2am, Wed & Thur 3pm-2am, Fri & Sat noon-3am, Sun noon-2am ⚥ Ⓥ

Specchio Magico
(5, D1) **$$$**
Italian
Calm and charming, this tiny Italian joint is perfect for intimate get-togethers and is the top Italian choice. Among the usual Italian fanfare, you can enjoy wonderfully soothing vegetable and chicken terrines in summer and the desserts are simply *fantisimo*.
✉ C/Luis Antúnez 3
☎ 93 415 33 71
Ⓜ Diagonal ⏲ Mon-Sat 2-4pm & 9-11pm ⚥ Ⓥ ♿ fair

THE SHORELINE

There are few stand-outs among the dozens of restaurants along the shoreline although most of them are reasonable enough. You may as well go for a wander and decide which one best suits your mood.

Can Solé
(4, K11) **$$$$**
Seafood
For a memorable meal, head to this century-old seafood restaurant where the selection is staggering, the food outstanding and the service little short of amazing – when you're half way through your fish, waiters saunter over, remove it, and discreetly strip away all the bones for you.
✉ C/Sant Carles 4, Barceloneta ☎ 93 221 50 12 Ⓜ Barceloneta ⏲ Mon-Sat 1-4pm & 8-11pm, Sun 1-4pm ⚥

Ruccola (3, J7) **$$$**
Catalan/Modern
Housed in the sterile and regrettably named World Trade Centre, this restaurant is one of the city's most fashionable, catering to local luminaries and their beautiful dates.

The views over the water are marvellous and the food – Catalan with the inevitable trendy Asian influences – is superb.
✉ World Trade Centre, Moll de Barcelona, Port Vell ☎ 93 508 82 68
Ⓜ Barceloneta ⏲ Mon-Sat 1-4pm & 8.30pm-midnight, Sun 1-4pm ⚥ Ⓥ ♿ excellent

7 Portes (4, G10) **$$$**
Catalan
Gilt-framed mirrors and black-and-white tiled floors reinforce the old world atmosphere of this Barcelona classic, founded in 1836 and renowned for its paella, seafood platters and enormous portions. You might sit in a chair previously warmed by the bum of Einsten, Orson Welles, Picasso or Ava Gardner.
✉ Pg d'Isabel II 14, Port Vell ☎ 93 319 30

33 Ⓜ Barceloneta ⏲ 1pm-1am ⚥ Ⓥ ♿ excellent

Xiringuito Escribà
(3, E11) **$$$$**
Seafood
Just because this beautiful beachside restaurant is run by the chocolate-making Escribà dynasty, don't rush through your main course. It could include sensational and varied paellas or hearty fish dinners. But do make sure you leave room to savour some of the most wickedly good chocolate cakes you'll ever taste. See p. 66 if you fancy buying some of Escribà's goodies.
✉ Ronda del Litoral 42, Port Olímpic
☎ 93 221 07 29
Ⓜ Ciutadella Vila Olímpica
⏲ Tues-Thur 11am-6pm, Fri & Sat 11am-6pm & 8pm-midnight ⚥ Ⓥ ♿ good

entertainment

Barcelona might be small but it's perfectly formed when it comes to putting on a show. The city is bursting with lively pubs, hedonistic gay bars and frenetic clubs, and the whirr of live jazz, rock, flamenco and salsa is never more than a short cab ride away. If symphonies and string quartets are more your thing, you can choose between venerable old music halls or snazzy high-tech auditoriums. The city is also a hotbed of contemporary dance and if that's too energetic for you, a host of cinemas offer everything from vanguard art house to Hollywood sha-la-la. What's more, the calendar is crammed with holidays and festivals, and Barcelonins are usually buzzing with the anticipation of an upcoming event.

But, whether you're hanging in a poky little bar or a colossal opera house, it's the vigour of the people in them that makes going out in Barcelona so exciting – the generous measures at the bar might possibly also be a factor. To experience the city in its natural light, you'll have to adjust to going out (much) later. Barcelonins are still in front of the mirror by the time you're usually in full flight; bars are empty until 11pm and clubbers don't even tap their feet before 2am.

Tickets & Listings

You can keep on top of all the goings-on by flicking through the weekly Spanish-language *Guía del Ocio* (€0.75), out on Thursday. Of the freebie mags distributed through bars and cafes, *Micro* and *Go Barcelona* have a good grip on what's happening on the club and music scene. For information on classical events, get the monthly *Informatiu Musical* leaflet, available through tourist offices; theatre buffs should check out the monthly listings guide *Teatre BCN*.

FNAC (4, B5; El Triangle, Plaça Catalunya 4) has a desk selling tickets for many events, especially musical ones, while the Palau de la Virreina arts information office (4, D5; La Rambla 99; ☎ 93 301 77 75) will see you right for classical events. Branches of La Caixa bank have machines called Servi-Caixa (information ☎ 902 10 12 12; **e** www.serviticket.com) where you can buy tickets for a wide range of events, including sport, using your credit card. You can also buy tickets over the counter at many branches.

Martin Hughes

SPECIAL EVENTS

January *New Year's Eve* – people eat a grape for each chime, for luck
Cavalcada dels Reis – 5 Jan; three kings arrive by sea and parade through the city
Festes dels Tres Tombs – 17 Jan; week-long festival in the district of Sant Antoni

February *Carnestoltes* – late Feb; parade and parties to open *carnaval* (carnival), coincides with **Festes de Santa Eulàlia**, the celebration of one of Barcelona's two patron saints with concerts and cultural events

April *Dia de Sant Jordi* – 23 Apr; the day of Catalunya's patron saint and the Day of the Book; men give women roses, women give men books
Feria de Abril – late Apr; ten days of Andalucían flamenco, food and carousing

May *Saló del Còmic* – early May; international comic fair at Estació de França
Sant Ponç – 11 May; quaint market in C/Hospital commemorating the patron saint of beekeepers and herbalists
Festa de la Diversitat – 11-13 May; harbour-front party celebrating multiculturalism
Festa de la Bicicleta – Sun in late May; thousands cycle around the city centre

June *L'Ou com Balla* – early to mid-June; 'dancing eggs' celebrates Corpus Christi
Sonar – June; a superb three-day music festival of electronica and multimedia
Dia per l'Alliberament Lesbià i Gai – late Jun; gay and lesbian festival and parade
Festa de la Musica – 21 Jun; free music concerts on the streets
Festival del Grec – June-Aug; city-wide performing arts festival
Nit del Foc – 23 June; fireworks, bonfires and merrymaking for the 'night of fire'

August *Festa Major de Gràcia* – mid-Aug; Gràcia's massive festival
Festa Major de Sants – late Aug; the festival of Sants

September *Diada* – 11 Sept; Catalan national day with flag-waving and speeches
Festa Major de la Barceloneta – late Sept; dancing and drinking in Barceloneta
Festes de la Mercè – 24 Sept; the big one, four days of festivities with music concerts, *castellers* (human castle builders), traditional folk dancing and parades of *gegants* (giants) and *capgrossos* (big heads) and a huge *correfoc* (fire race)
Mostra de Vins i Caves de Catalunya – 24 Sept; four-day food and wine festival in the Penedès wine region

October *Festival International de Jazz de Barcelona* – Oct-Dec; jazz around the city

November *Fira del Disc de Col.leccionista* – early Nov; Europe's largest second-hand record fair

December *Fira de Santa Llúcia* – 1-24 Dec; Christmas market by the Catedral

Damien Simons

BARS

Barri Gòtic is the traditional jumping-off point with lots of lively bars and favourite clubs, while El Raval has many grungy and charismatic drinking dens. El Borne, where you'll find stacks of trendy late-night bars to kick off the evening, is currently unstoppable as the hippest and most stylish part of town, while chic designer bars abound in uptown l'Eixample.

Bar Almirall (4, C3)

People have been boozing here since 1860, which makes it the oldest continuously functioning bar in Barcelona. Delightfully dishevelled, it still has its original bar, much loved by punters and loathed by staff. ✉ C/de Joaquím Costa 33 Ⓜ Universitat ⊙ 7pm-2.30am (until 3am Fri & Sat)

Bar Pastis (4, G5)

No bigger than a postage stamp, this bar was opened after WWII by a Catalan couple infatuated with Marseilles. They dedicated it to French cabaret, had only Edith Piaff on the stereo and a drinks list comprising of pastis. There are more drinks on offer these days but the character remains the same. ✉ C/de Santa Mònica 4 ☎ 93 318 79 80 Ⓜ Drassanes ⊙ 7.30pm-2.30am (until 3am Fri & Sat)

Barcelona Pipa Club

(4, F6) Ring the buzzer at one of the best all-night bars you'll ever know. It's a genuine pipe smokers club by day and is transformed into a dim, laidback and incurably cool bar at night. King Juan Carlos could walk in and drop his pants and nobody would bat an eye. ✉ Plaça Reial 3 ☎ 93 302 47 32 Ⓜ Liceu ⊙ 10pm-6am

Boadas 1 (4, B5)

The founder of this 1933 Art Deco cocktail bar learned his craft serving Hemingway in the famed Floridita Bar in Havana. The walls are covered with mementoes, including a sketch by Miró, of the contented customers who've gotten sloshed on the hundreds of enticing cocktails on offer here. ✉ C/dels Tallers 1 ☎ 93 318 95 92 Ⓜ Catalunya ⊙ Mon-Sat noon-3am

Café Royale (4, F6)

These are some of the most sought after sofas in Barcelona, perfect for chilling out with warm lighting, a good-looking crowd, and irresistible soul, funk and bossa fusions. It gets terribly packed with visitors at the weekend. ✉ C/Nou de Zurbano 3 ☎ 93 317 61 24 Ⓜ Liceu ⊙ Tues-Sat 5pm-2.30am (until 3am Fri & Sat)

La Vinya del Senyor

(4, F10) A wine-taster's fantasy, this bar has a stunning location looking out over the Santa Maria del Mar church. You can choose from almost 300 varieties of wine and cava from around the world and enjoy inventive *platillos* (mini-tapas) as you sip. The table by the window upstairs provides one of the best views

in the city. ✉ Plaça de Santa Maria del Mar 5 ☎ 93 310 33 79 Ⓜ Jaume I ⊙ Tues-Sun noon-1.30pm

Las Guitarres (5, B1)

Cramped and crumbling, this unique bar is like a time capsule devoted to music. It has more than 200 guitars, kept in tune for your strumming satisfaction, hanging from the roof and cassettes of crackling classic jazz compete with the disregarded ticking of several grandfather clocks. There are no signs so look for the poster of Afghanistan on the door. ✉ Rambla de Prat 9 ☎ 93 227 87 81 Ⓜ Fontana ⊙ 6.30pm-12.30am

Les Gens Que L'Aime Pub (5, H3)

Incurably romantic, this basement bar in l'Eixample combines antique red velvet sofas, candle lighting, dark woods and privacy – perfect for a night of sweet nothings. ✉ C/de València 286 ☎ 93 215 68 79 Ⓜ Passeig de Gràcia ⊙ 6pm-2.30am (until 3am Fri & Sat)

London Bar (4, G4)

On the edge of the once notorious Barrio Xinés, this bar was founded in 1910 as a hangout for circus hands and drew the likes of Picasso and Miró in search

of local colour. You can still find the entire palate of El Raval, and the mirrored walls and Modernista touches provide the backdrop for the lively mingling of locals and travellers.
✉ C/Nou de la Rambla 34 ☎ 93 318 52 61
e tonoyeli@eresmas.com Ⓜ Liceu ◷ Tues-Sun 7pm-4am (until 5am Fri & Sat)

Marcela (4, F4)
This place has been in the same family for five generations and looks like it hasn't had a lick of paint since it was first opened in 1820. Assorted chandeliers, tiles and mirrors decorate its one big room which, on weekends, is packed to its rickety rafters with a cheerful mishmash of shady characters, drag queens and slumming uptowners.
✉ C/de Sant Pau 65
☎ 93 442 72 63
Ⓜ Liceu ◷ Mon-Sat 10pm-2am (until 3am Fri & Sat)

Mirablau (2, A4)
For the most stunning views of Barcelona – and the spectacle of the city's rich and famous dancing badly – catch a cab to this chi-chi bar and club

perched on top of Tibidabo. Doormen come on for the club at 11pm and it helps if you're wearing coloured corduroys or Prada.
✉ Plaça del Doctor Andreu ☎ 93 418 58 79 🚃 FGC Tibidabo, then Tramvia Blau or take a taxi ◷ bar 11am-11pm; club 11pm-4.30am (until 5am Fri & Sat)

Palau Dalmases (4, E10) Perhaps the most pretentious bar in town, this 'baroque space' occupies a handsome 14th-century palace and is awash with period splendour (or naff bric-a-brac, depending on your mood). Drinks are limited to wine and punch, and prices are futuristic.
✉ C/de Montcada 20
☎ 93 310 06 73
Ⓜ Jaume I ◷ Tues-Sat 8pm-2am, Sun 6-10pm

Parnasse (4, G8)
This colourful, laid-back bar is a hangout for puppeteers and has a couple of vegetarians camped on a bench in the corner. It specialises in drinks you'll be pushed to find elsewhere, including absinthe, and the warmest welcome you'll get before

going home.
✉ C/d'En Gignàs 21
☎ 93 310 12 47
Ⓜ Jaume I ◷ Tues-Sun 8pm-3am

Partycular (2, A4)
Sophisticated and stylish, this colossal bar is set inside a hacienda on top of Tibidabo with beautiful rambling gardens and views over the funfair and city. Fun all year round, it's a must in summer when bars are sprinkled throughout the gardens and seduction is in the air.
✉ Avda Tibidabo 61
☎ 93 211 62 61
🚃 take a taxi ◷ Wed & Thur 6.30pm-2.30am, Fri & Sat midnight-3am

Pilè 43 (4, G7)
This cool retro bar doubles as an equally cool retro furniture and design shop. Everything in it, from the chair you sit in to the glass you've stained with lippy, is on sale. With a bit of luck your table won't be bought from under you before your cocktail or tasty vegetarian snacks arrive.
✉ C/de n'Aglá 4
☎ 93 317 39 02
Ⓜ Liceu ◷ Mon-Sat 1.30-4.30pm & 7pm-2am (until 3am Fri & Sat)

Pitin Bar (4, E11)
Although the area of El Borne goes in and out of fashion, this stylish and welcoming bar has remained an outpost of cool for decades. Up the spiralling staircase is the perfect spot to launch yourself into a big night.
✉ Pg del Born 34
☎ 93 310 19 60
Ⓜ Jaume I
◷ 6pm-2am

Mojitos & Measures
Cocktails are the weekend drink of the masses on 'la marche' in Barcelona and the invigorating Cuban mojito is a universal favourite. For our money, **Stingers Cocktails** (5, F2; cnr of C/de Corsega and C/de Pau Claris; ☎ 93 217 71 87; Mon-Sat 6.30pm-3am) in l'Eixample does the best mojito in the metropolis. Here's their recipe, which you *will* want to try when you get home: a jigger-and-a-half of white rum, ½ teaspoon of white sugar, juice of half a lime, a dribble of angostura bitters and crushed ice. Mix well, add loads of fresh mint and serve without excuse.

DANCE CLUBS

Benidorm (4, B3)
Nothing like the name might suggest, this is a harmonious and eye-catching little club that's low in light and rich in ambience. It purrs to the smooth sounds of local and international DJs.
✉ C/de Joaquim Costa 39 ☎ 93 317 80 52 Ⓜ Universitat or Sant Antoni ⏰ 7pm-2am ⑤ free

Dot (4, G7)
This little treasure, in the back streets of Barri Gòtic, glows everyday of the week. There's a red-lit bar at the front for a chat or a snuggle and a small, congenial dance floor out back, which is awash with projections of cult movies.
✉ C/Nou de Sant Francesc ☎ 93 302 70 26 Ⓔ www.dotlightclub.com Ⓜ Drassanes ⏰ 10pm-2.30am ⑤ free

Fonfone (4, G6)
For the atmosphere of a club without the cover charge, get a feel for Fonfone with its cool and colourful design, relaxed door policy and right-on-the-minute choons. It's more like a bar before 1am.
✉ C/dels Escudellers 24 ☎ 93 317 14 24 Ⓜ Drassanes ⏰ 10pm-2.30am ⑤ free

KGB (3, B5)
When your party's running out of puff, head to this grim industrial warehouse, where the staple of house and techno gets harder and harder as morning gets nearer and nearer, until it eventually beats the crap out of you

Party Port
If bumping and grinding against sweaty torsos and scantily clad dancers is your thing, head down to Port Olímpic (3, F10) after midnight on weekends, where stacks of indistinguishable clubs provide pumping Spanish chart hits to testosterone-laden men and out-numbered women determined to party.

and dumps your racked and broken body at the door at dawn. The dress code is as loose as the music is tight.
✉ C/de Ca l'Alegre de Dalt 55 ☎ 93 210 59 06 Ⓜ Joanic ⏰ Thur-Sat 9pm-6am ⑤ €6 (incl 1st drink)

Moog (4, G5)
Moog (named after the synthesiser) is reliable for techno and electronica, and is always packed with a young and enthusiastic crowd. Bigger in stature than it is in size, it attracts lots of big name DJs. Upstairs specialises in retro Latin dance.
✉ L'Arc del Teatre 3 ☎ 93 318 59 66 Ⓔ www.masimas.com Ⓜ Drassanes ⏰ 11.30pm-5am ⑤ €6

Otto Zutz (3, C3)
This converted three-storey

warehouse used to be the hippest club in Barcelona, patronised by international stars of every ilk. Inevitably, the wannabees and expensive dressers have replaced the celebrities but the gritty elegance remains and this is still a great place to dance. There's a different vibe on the three floors (top floor VIPs only), linked by a giant atrium.
✉ C/de Lincoln 15 ☎ 93 238 07 22 Ⓜ FGC Gràcia ⏰ Tues-Sat 11am-6am ⑤ €10

Row Club (5, F1)
Run by the Sonar Festival organisers, this classic club takes over the Philippe Starck-furnished Nick Havanna's – a huge 1980s retro bar – at the weekend and fills it with the best local and international DJs spinning deep house,

Martin Hughes

Dance the night (and day) away...

techno and front line electronica.

✉ Nick Havanna's, C/del Rosselló 208
☎ 93 215 65 91
ⓔ www.rowclub.com
Ⓜ Diagonal ⏰ Thur-Sat 11.30pm-5.30am
Ⓢ €9 (incl 1 drink)

Terrazza (1, A1)

Move to 'the terrace' for rejuvenation when you run out of steam. Some of the biggest international names play at this summertime must, which can be relied on for some of the meatiest dance tunes on vinyl. In winter it moves indoors and becomes the Discothèque.

✉ Avda del Marquès de Comillas (behind Poble Espanyol)
☎ 93 423 12 85
ⓔ www.nightsun group.com Ⓜ Espanya
⏰ mid-May-Oct midnight-6am Ⓢ €14

La Paloma

The 100-year-old La Paloma (4, B2; C/del Tigre 27; ☎ 93 301 68 97; Ⓜ Universitat) is a unique local institution and an essential night out in Barcelona. It opens 11pm to 5am Thursday to Saturday; admission is €5. The evening starts with 'the band' playing cha-chas and tangos to a chirpy crowd of mostly middle-aged couples. At 1am it transforms into the Bongo Lounge when DJs take over and the beautiful young things stream in. The music gets harder as the night wears on but you can still see 60-year-old senoritas flashing bits of leg in impromptu can-cans. Catch the last half hour of the band (avoiding the queues) and clinch a table along the balcony to admire the faded grandeur of the room.

Torres de Ávila

(1, A1) Housed inside the tall entrance towers of the Poble Espanyol, this kooky club is the culmination of the designer bar phenomenon that swept through Barcelona in the 1980s and is full of surreal features. It's the stone, iron and glass creation of local designer Javier Mariscal (he of Cobi, the Olympic mascot).

✉ entrance to Poble Espanyol, Avda del Marquès de Comillas
☎ 93 424 93 09
ⓔ www.welcome.to/ torresdeavila
Ⓜ Espanya ⏰ Fri & Sat 12.30pm-7am Ⓢ €9

CINEMAS

Films shown in their original languages with subtitles are identified by the letters VO (*versió original*). Getting a ticket at the door will only be a problem on weekend evenings and you can get advance tickets through Servi-Caixa (see p. 87). Monday is usually discount night.

Casablanca (5, E1)

The films (non-mainstream and art house) shown on these screens are generally worth a look. The only problem is that the seats are perversely uncomfortable and no amount of popcorn can take your mind off it.

✉ Pg de Gràcia 115
☎ 93 218 43 45
Ⓜ Diagonal ⏰ 8.30pm & 10.30pm Ⓢ €5 (Mon €3.50)

Filmoteca (3, E2)

This government-funded gem specialises in programmes that group films together by particular directors, styles, eras and countries. Some films may be decades old while others are still in the cinemas. Programmes change daily – get the fortnightly schedules directly from the cinema.

✉ Avda de Sarrià 31
☎ 93 410 75 70
Ⓜ Hospital Clinic ⏰ 5pm, 7.30pm & 10pm Ⓢ €2-2.70
🧒 5pm most days for children's shows

Icària-Yelmo (3, E10)

Behind the Port Olímpic, this is a typical multiplex with 15 screens predominantly devoted to mainstream but with a sprinkling of alternative flicks. This is a good option when you need to amuse the kids.

✉ C/de Salvador Espriu 61 ☎ 93 221 75 85
ⓔ www.yelmocineplex .es Ⓜ Ciutadella Vila Olímpica ⏰ 7.30pm & 10.15pm (plus midnight Fri & Sat) Ⓢ €5.25 (Mon €3.75) 🧒

IMAX (4, K9)
When there is a decent flick made for this screen format – apart from nature documentaries – this will be a great place to see it. It offers a choice of formats including OMNIMAX and 3D. Most of the documentaries are VO.
✉ Moll d'Espanya
☎ 902 33 22 11
Ⓜ Barceloneta
⏲ Mon-Fri 12.30pm-11.30pm; Sat, Sun & hols 10.30am-11.45pm
⑤ €7 ♿ varies

Méliès Cinemes (3, F4)
This two-screen movie house specialises in showing original versions of old classics and sometimes fills the gap between the dry intellectualism of Filmoteca and the Hollywood excesses of the multiplexes.
✉ C/de Villarroel 102
☎ 93 451 00 51
Ⓜ Urgell ⏲ 8.30pm & 10.30pm ⑤ €3.60 (Mon €2.40)

Verdi (3, C4)
This cinematic institution is highly regarded for championing creations left of centre and was the first to specialise in VO. It recently expanded into the Verdi Park and you can now choose from nine screens.
✉ C/de Verdi 32 (Verdi Park Torrijos 49) ☎ 93 237 05 16 (Verdi Park 93 238 79 90) Ⓜ Fontana
⏲ 8.30pm & 10.45pm (plus midnight Fri & Sat)
⑤ €5.25 (Mon €4)
♿ Verdi Park only

LIVE MUSIC VENUES

Abaixadors Deu
(4, F10) This multipurpose venue is in the heart of El Borne and reflects the style and dynamism of the precinct. You could get anything from punk to poetry so swing past the relaxed bar, the Lounge Social Club, to pick up a programme. Across the road, Astin is a hip little bar that largely features local rock.
✉ Abaixadors 10, just off Plaça de Santa Maria del Mar ☎ 93 268 10 19 Ⓜ Jaume I
⏲ Wed-Sun 11pm-3am, Fri & Sat 11pm-4am ⑤ varies

Apolo (4, H2)
It's well worth checking out what's on at this busy and atmospheric old music hall. An eclectic programme of gigs ranges from world music to touring rock bands that you'll never again see in a venue so cosy. After the encores, shirty security staff clear the hall for the 'Nitsaclub' dance bash.
✉ C/Nou de la Rambla 113 ☎ 93 441 40 01
📧 www.nitsa.com

Ⓜ Paral.lel ⏲ gigs around 10pm, Nitsaclub Fri & Sat midnight-6am ⑤ €7-15, Nitsaclub €11 (incl 1 drink)

Bikini (2, F5)
The reincarnation of a legendary club, that was torn down in 1990 to make way for a shopping mall, the modern Bikini is regarded by many as the best venue in Barcelona with crisp acoustics and diverse programming.
✉ C/Deu i Mata 105, Les Corts ☎ 93 322 08 00 📧 www.bikinibcn .com Ⓜ Les Corts
⏲ Tues-Sat midnight-4.30am, Fri & Sat midnight-5.30am ⑤ €9 (incl your 2nd drink)

Garatge Club (3, C11)
If bristling guitars and uncompromising indie ring your bell, then 'the garage' is the place for you. Depending on your luck you could get anything from ska or speed metal to a closed door (so check first).
✉ C/de Pallars 195, Poblenou

☎ 93 309 14 38
Ⓜ Llacuna ⏲ Fri & Sat midnight-5am ⑤ varies

Harlem Jazz Club
(4, F8) Deep in the Barri Gòtic, this is a stalwart of the local scene and the first stop for jazz aficionados. Nightly sessions (except Monday) include traditional and contemporary jazz, along with creative fusions from around the world. The scarcity of tables contributes to the club's relaxed and friendly atmosphere.
✉ Comtessa de Sobradiel 8 ☎ 93 310 07 55 Ⓜ Jaume I
⏲ Tues-Sun 8pm-4am (gigs usually 11pm-2am) ⑤ up to €8 (incl 1 drink)

Martin Hughes

Jamboree (4, F6)
Better as a pulsating gig venue than the club it turns into afterwards, this wildly popular cellar hosts local and international names in everything from jazz to hip hop. The club – cranking R&B and soul downstairs and Latin fusion up top – attracts some dodgy looking characters at the weekend. Its Sunday night blues sessions are a perfect end to the weekend.
⊠ Plaça Reial 17
☎ 93 301 75 64
ⓔ www.masimas.com
Ⓜ Liceu ⏱ 2pm-5am (gigs around 11pm)
Ⓢ approx €11 (incl 1 drink)

Jazz Si Club (4, D1)
If you want to see who'll be playing at the other venues next time you visit, head to this delightfully disordered club cafe run by a contemporary music school. It's a meeting place for musos with diverse live music every night.
⊠ C/Requesens 2
☎ 93 329 00 20
Ⓜ Sant Antoni
⏱ 9pm-3am Ⓢ free to €5

La Boîte (3, E2)
A local institution and a must for jazz, soul and blues fans, this highly regarded uptown basement was the first music venue of the entrepreneurial Mas Brothers, doyens of the local entertainment scene.
⊠ Avda Diagonal 477
☎ 93 419 59 50 or 93 319 17 89
ⓔ www.masimas.com
Ⓜ Diagonal ⏱ 11pm-5.30am, gigs midnight
Ⓢ €7-15

Luz de Gas (3, D2)
Anything goes at this large

and happening music hall that hosts residencies and big international names from the worlds of soul, country, salsa, rock, jazz, pop and cabaret in a beautiful belle epoch setting.
⊠ C/de Muntaner 246
☎ 93 209 77 11
🚆 FGC Muntaner or take a taxi ⏱ gigs 10pm until late Ⓢ free to €9

Sidecar (4, F6)
Just off Plaça Reial, this basement has a friendly underground vibe and is the place for the best of local indie with some occasional touring treats. After gigs, there's pool and late night fringe shows from local performers and artists.
⊠ C/les Heures 4-6
☎ 93 302 15 86
Ⓜ Liceu ⏱ Tues-Sat 10pm-3am Ⓢ €6 (incl 1 drink)

FOLK & LATIN DANCE

Antilla Barcelona
(3, G3) Never mind if you don't know your salsa from your spicy tomato sauce, if you arrive early at this Latin club on Friday and Saturday, you can get free lessons before great bands take over for the rest of the evening.
⊠ C/d'Aragò 141
☎ 93 451 21 51
Ⓜ Hospital Clinic
⏱ Sun-Thur 11pm-4am, Fri & Sat 11pm-5am
Ⓢ €10 (incl 1 drink)

Los Tarantos (4, F6)
Upstairs of the Jamboree (see above) you'll find locals and tourists getting hot and steamy with flamenco, Latin and salsa sessions. As well as the long-established Flamenco

tablao (show), you can catch the occasional concert. Afterwards, the theme carries on with the club's irresistible Latin mix.
⊠ Plaça Reial 17
☎ 93 389 16 61
Ⓜ Liceu ⏱ 9.30pm-5am, Mon-Sat flamenco tablao 10-10.30pm
Ⓢ €25 (incl 2 drinks) ♿

Tablao de Carmen
(1, A1) A very swanky and lively flamenco show with a full complement of guitarists, singers and dancers. It's not as touristy as you might expect, dinner is half decent, and you can save yourself the entrance fee to Poble Espanyol if you book in advance.
⊠ Arcs 9, Poble

Espanyol ☎ 93 325 68 95 ⓔ www.tablao decarmen.com
Ⓜ Plaça Espanya
⏱ shows Tues-Sun 9.30pm Ⓢ entry to Poble Espanyol €6; show with drink €27; show with dinner €50

Terrasamba (3, C4)
Anyone into this lively brand of Brazilian ballroom should dress to sweat at this samba club, which gives free lessons on Wednesdays. Nobody will mind if you blame your two left feet on one too many of their caipirinha cocktails.
⊠ C/de la Perla 34
Ⓜ Fontana ⏱ 9pm-3am Tues-Sun Ⓢ free

Sardana – the Catalan Folk Dance

Catalans take their national dance, the *sardana*, very seriously. While it's not very exciting to watch – just a lot of holding hands, bobbing up and down, and the occasional step to the left and back again – it's a strong affirmation of Catalan identity and therefore fascinating to watch on Catalan soil. The music, in turns melancholic and jolly, is played by a reed and brass band called a *cobla* and most of it was written by the 19th century. The origins of the dance are unclear but the first written reference was in the 16th century.

Sardanas are danced at all traditional festivals but the best place to see it is in front of the Catedral (Sat noon-2pm, Sun 6.30-8.30pm). Crowds of mostly elderly folk gather in ever widening circles and dance around their bags. It's not as easy as it looks and you shouldn't join a circle above your class or break up a couple, lest you incur the wrath of the dancers.

Martin Hughes

CLASSICAL MUSIC, OPERA, DANCE & THEATRE

Ciutat del Teatre

(3, J4) The 'city of theatre' is an ambitious new arts complex incorporating Barcelona's theatre school and several highly regarded theatres including the Teatre Mercat de les Flors (in the old flower market) next door. It specialises in progressive and inexpensive student productions and shares its space with visiting shows and other performing arts.
✉ **Plaça Margarida Xirgu** ☎ **93 227 39 00**
e **www.diba.es/iteatre/**
⑩ **Espanya**
🕐 box office two hours

before performance
⑧ €10-12

Gran Teatre del Liceu

(4, F5) Promoted as one of the most technologically advanced theatres in the world, the reconstructed opera house (the original was destroyed by fire in 1994) is a fabulously plush setting for your favourite aria. World-class dance companies also strut their stuff across its esteemed stage, which also sometimes plays host to classical musical concerts as well.
✉ **La Rambla 51-59**

☎ **93 485 99 13**
e **www.liceubarcelona**
.com ⑩ **Liceu** 🕐 box office Mon-Fri 10am-1pm & 3-7pm ⑧ varies
⚲ matinees for kids occasionally

L'Auditori (3, D8)

The permanent home of Barcelona's symphony orchestra (known as OBC) is a starkly modern, and relatively new, pleasure dome for serious music lovers. Its comfortable (and acoustically unrivalled) main auditorium hosts orchestral and chamber music throughout the year as well as occasional world music jams.

✉ C/de Lepant 150
☎ 93 247 93 00
e www.auditori.com
Ⓜ Marina ⏱ box office 10am-9pm
⑤ varies ♿ matinees at 11am

L'Espai de Danza
(3, D3) This government-sponsored space is a show-case for the performing arts in Catalunya and concentrates on an extensive programme of contemporary dance. Classical and experimental groups also hit their straps here and there's occasionally music without movement.

✉ Travessera de Gràcia 63 ☎ 93 414 31 33
e cultura.gencat.es/espai/ Ⓜ Diagonal
⏱ box office Tues-Sat 6.30-9.30pm, Sun 5-7pm Sun ⑤ average €9

Palau de la Música Catalana (4, B9)
Still the main venue for classical, choral and chamber music, this Modernista masterpiece hosts an extensive programme ranging from young, local ensembles to international orchestras. It is visually stunning but acoustically inferior although continuing renovations and extensions are improving the venue all the time.

✉ C/de Sant Pere més Alt 11 ☎ 93 295 72 00
e www.palaumusica.org Ⓜ Urquinaona
⏱ box office Mon-Sat 10am-9pm, 1hr before Sun performance
⑤ varies ♿

Sala Beckett (3, B5)
Founded by the renowned Catalan playwright José

The grand Gran Teatre del Liceu (p. 95)

Sanchis Sinisterra, this theatre company (named with the consent of the Irish Nobel laureate) offers experimental work from Catalunya and around Spain, as well as occasional contemporary dance performances.

✉ C/de ca l'Alegre de Dalt 55 bis ☎ 93 284 53 12 e www.teatral.net/beckett Ⓜ Joanic
⏱ information Mon-Fri 10am-2pm & 4-8pm
⑤ €12-15

Teatre Lliure (3, C4)
The most prestigious theatre group working in Catalan today, this company is renowned for turning its hand to just about anything and with flair. Expect the works, from Anglo classics to the vanguard indigenous productions. Performances are on a stage in the middle of the theatre, surrounded by the audience.

✉ C/Montseny 47
☎ 93 218 92 51
e www.teatrelliure.com Ⓜ Fontana
⏱ 9pm Tues-Sat, box office from 5pm
⑤ €12-15

Teatre Malic (4, E11)
This tiny 60-seater in an

El Borne basement offers a packed programme including music, alternative theatre, experimental pieces of established local talent and first-runs from emerging geniuses.

✉ C/de la Fusina 3
☎ 93 310 70 35
Ⓜ Barceloneta
⏱ shows usually 9pm, box office from 7pm
⑤ €12 ♿

Teatre Nacional de Catalunya (3, C8)
Funded by the city council and designed to be *the* home of Catalan theatre, this expensive high-tech venue opened its doors in 1997 amid controversy. In its first couple of years it was attacked by critics for being too commercial but it now seems to have got its house in order and is a wonderful showcase for performing arts from all over Catalunya. Home to the Teatre Romea company.

✉ Plaça de les Arts 1
☎ 93 306 57 06 or 93 306 57 00
e www.tnc.es
Ⓜ Glòries ⏱ Tues-Sat 9pm, Sun 6pm; box office Mon noon-3pm & 4-9pm, Tues-Sat noon-9pm, Sun noon-6pm Sun ⑤ €16-20 ♿

GAY & LESBIAN BARCELONA

Arena Madre (5, K1)
Arenas abound in gay Barcelona and the name is used for three different clubs and a cinema. This place is where the young crowd goes cruising to a throbbing soundtrack of house, garage and techno, with a long dance floor and a 'dark room'.
✉ C/de Balmes 32
☎ 93 487 83 42
e www.arenadisco.com Ⓜ Universitat
⏰ Tues-Sun midnight-5am Ⓢ €4.50 (incl 1 drink)

Bahía (5, E1)
A good port of call for visiting lesbians, this convivial Gothic bar draws everyone from butch dykes to the girls next door, and is a good spot for socialising with the locals.
✉ C/Sèneca 12
Ⓜ Diagonal ⏰ 10pm-3am Ⓢ free

Café Nou-3 (4, C4)
This mixed gay bar almost manages to make walls lined with vinyl covers seem stylish. Although friendly, there's not much life here until after 1am but you can keep yourself entertained with an electronic dartboard and the 1970s and '80s vinyl that's stacked up on the bar waiting to be requested.
✉ C/de Doctor Dou 12
☎ 93 412 08 47
Ⓜ Catalunya
⏰ 8pm-3am

Dietrich (3, F4)
This divinely glam corner of l'Eixample is big and friendly, and full of pretty professionals. It touts itself as a theatre cafe and hosts some of the best drag in the city.
✉ C/del Consell de Cent 255 ☎ 93 451 77 07 Ⓜ Universitat
⏰ Mon-Thur 10.30pm-2am, Fri & Sat 10.30pm-3am, Sun 6pm-2.30am Ⓢ free

Medusa & Zeltas Club (3, F4)
Standing shoulder-to-shoulder, these two terrific bars provide a top night out with comfy couches, lots of space and deep funky grooves. There's a universal welcome at Zeltas while only boys get the nod when Medusa is busy.
✉ C/de Casanova 73-75 ☎ Medusa 93 454 53 63, Zeltas 93 454 19 02
e www.medusacafe.com Ⓜ Urgell
⏰ Medusa 11pm-3am; Zeltas Wed-Sat 11pm-3am Ⓢ free to both

Metro (4, A2)
Both dance floors of the city's biggest and busiest gay club are absolutely heaving at weekends (and for weekday theme nights) when a largely gay crowd thumps to top-of-the-range house and techno. During the week it's dance club pop and handbags ahoy, and is generally too gay for many.
✉ C/de Sepúlveda 185, nr Plaça de la Universitat ☎ 93 323 52 27 Ⓜ Universitat
⏰ Sun-Thur midnight-5am, Fri & Sat midnight-6am Ⓢ €10

New Chaps (5, F2)
As the name suggests, this bar is strictly for chaps – mostly mature, macho and suitably hirsute. It attracts a regular jean- and leather-clad posse, and has theme nights and a shadowy downstairs.
✉ Avda Diagonal 365 ☎ 93 215 53 65
Ⓜ Diagonal or Verdaguer ⏰ 9pm-3am Ⓢ free

Punto BCN (3, F4)
A classic for pre- or postprandial drinks among a relaxed 30-something crowd of all shapes and sizes. It's extremely popular and one of the few gay get-togethers that opens early. A large upstairs seating area allows you to survey the talent below .
✉ C/de Muntaner 63-65 ☎ 93 453 61 23
Ⓜ Universitat ⏰ 6pm-2.30am Ⓢ free

Salvation (4, A9)
Flavour of the month, again, Salvation is the place for a big happy blow-out with two big dance floors offering house and chart for wiggling and watching. The gleaming torsos of the staff are part of the attraction but it's strictly no touching.
✉ Ronda de Sant Pere 19-21 ☎ 93 318 06 86
e www.matineegroup.com Ⓜ Urquinaona
⏰ midnight-5am
Ⓢ €10

Sauna Casanova (3, F4) There are stacks of gay saunas around the city centre. This one is the most central and can provide details of the others.
✉ C/de Casanova 57
☎ 93 323 78 60
Ⓜ Urgell ⏰ 24hrs
Ⓢ €10

SPECTATOR SPORTS

Football

Football is far and away the most popular spectator sport in the city and **Barça**, the main club, is one of the biggest in the world (see pp. 14-15). Camp Nou sees plenty of European action in autumn. It is much easier to get tickets (€20-45) to see the city's second club, first-division rivals **Espanyol** (☎ 93 292 77 00; [e] www.rcdespanyol.com) at Estadi Olímpic (1, B3; Avda de l'Estadi, Montjuïc; Ⓜ Paral.lel, then Funicular to Montjuïc) but it doesn't have anywhere near the same atmosphere. There are also a few other local clubs that play in the lower divisions.

Basketball

After football, this is the second most popular spectator sport and two local teams, **Club Joventut Badalona** (☎ 93 460 20 40; [e] www.penya.com) and **FC Barcelona** (yes, part of the football club; ☎ 93 496 36 75), stand shoulder to shoulder among the best in Europe. Club has the edge over FC because it has won the European Basketball Cup although FC has been in the finals five times. FC plays on Saturday night and Sunday afternoon at the Palau Blaugrana (2, H3) in Les Corts and Club play way out in the suburbs of Badalona.

Pillars of the Community

If you're in town when there's a *festa major* (festival) on, you'll come across the curious Catalan tradition of *castells* (human castles), mobile monuments to civic spirit and teamwork. The sport – for it is passionately regarded as such – is popular throughout Catalunya with more than 60 *colles* (teams) competing at competitions and festivals. The golden age of castells was in the 1880s when one daring community reached the record of 10 levels, a feat not repeated until 1998. If all goes well, the castell is completed when an *anxaneta*, usually a little kid with balls as big as his head, clambers to the top and then gives a nervous wave to the relieved crowd, the signal to start whooping with abandon.

Ice & Roller Hockey

FC Barcelona incorporates the two local teams in these sports. Ice hockey is still at a nascent stage and tickets for league games are generally free. Roller hockey has long been popular throughout Catalunya and FC Barcelona plays at the Palau Blaugrana (2, H3) indoor arena beside Camp Nou.

American Football

Yes, American football enjoys healthy support here. Attendances to see the **Barcelona Dragons** (☎ 93 425 49 49; **e** www.dragons.es) average over 10,000. The Dragons are big fish in the small European League pond and play on weekend evenings from April to June at Estadi Olímpic (see Football for details) accompanied by lots of glitz and razzmatazz. Tickets cost €7.50.

Motor Sports

The motor racing circuit at Montmeló, 20km outside the city, hosts the Spanish Grand Prix in late April/early May and a motorcycle Grand Prix in June. The bikes have become very popular in recent years, thanks largely to the revving success of Catalans Alex Crivillè and Carles Checa on the 500cc circuit. Contact Circuit de Catalunya at C/de Parets del Vallès a Granollers, Montmeló (☎ 93 571 97 00; **e** www.circuitcat.com) for details. Tickets are available from Servi-Caixa (see p. 87).

Tennis

The most prestigious event in Barcelona's tennis calendar – and one which attracts many of the world's top players – is the **Trofeig Comte de Godò** tournament, which is held in late April at the Reial Club de Tennis Barcelona (2, D2; Bosch i Gimpera 5, Les Corts; ☎ 93 208 78 52; **e** www.rctb1899.es; **[FGC]** FGC Reina Elisenda). Tickets are available from 9am to 6pm during competitions and cost €18 to €60 for the Trofeig Comte de Godò tournament.

Bullfighting

Catalans generally don't like bull-fighting but if you must you can watch events at 6pm on Sunday during the summer months at the Plaça Braus Monumental (3, C8; **M** Monumental). Tickets cost between €15 and €75, and are available at the arena (Wed-Sat 10.30am-2pm & 6-7pm). Call ☎ 902 33 22 11 for details.

Martin Hughes

Fancy your chances?

places to stay

The 1992 Olympics began a boom in the construction of new hotels in Barcelona that hasn't let up since. But the number of new beds can hardly keep up with the increasing demand as Barcelona has raced to become one of the world's most popular destinations. While there are good hotels in every price bracket throughout the city, you'll be seriously limited for choice unless you book well in advance. Many perennial favourites are booked out months ahead so you had better get your skates on.

Traditionally, the favourite address for visitors is La Rambla, where there's a host of different lodgings to fit every budget. If you stay on this strip, though, you'll be paying in part for the prestigious location and will get more comfort for your buck elsewhere.

Room Rates

The price ranges in this chapter indicate the cost per night of a standard double room and are merely meant as guidelines. The reviews assess the character and facilities of each place within the context of the price bracket.

Deluxe	over €200
Top End	€100-200
Mid-Range	€40-100
Budget	under €40

The city's accommodation is divided into two categories: hotels (H) and hostals (Hs). Signs (white letters on a blue background) outside each lodging indicate its status. The only clear-cut difference is that every room in a hotel must have en suite facilities. All hotel rates are subject to a 7% value-added tax known as IVA.

If you roll into town without a reservation, head straight to the tourist office on Plaça Catalunya (4, A7), which, even at the busiest times, can usually find you shelter. However, you can't afford to be blase about this service because you could end up being shunted around from one place to another out in the suburbs, or with no room at all.

Because of Barcelona's popularity with tourists and business travellers, there's hardly such thing as a low season. Hotels that normally cater largely for professionals often offer discounts at Christmas, Easter and during the summer when there is less business activity. Otherwise, January and February is a relatively quiet time when you might be able to negotiate yourself a better deal.

Martin Hughes

Open sesame at the Hotel Claris

DELUXE

Hotel Arts (3, F10)

Barcelona's most fashionable hotel is in a skyscraper overlooking the beach. Designed by renowned US architects Skidmore, Owings and Merrill, it is required shelter for readers of *wallpaper** magazine. All the rooms are superbly equipped and decorated with original art, but it has an impersonal atmosphere and is not nearly as flash as the disciples of style make out.
✉ **Marina 19-21, Port Olimpic ☎ 93 221 10 00; fax 93 221 10 70** ⓔ **www.ritzcarlton .com** Ⓜ **Ciutadella Vila Olimpica** ✕ ♿ ♿ **excellent**

Hotel Claris (5, G3)

This is the best lobby in the city in which to pretend you're a recalcitrant rock star. It's also the best hotel in Barcelona: a 1930s postmodern delight combining marble, steel and glass. Unhassled staff cater to your every whim, two outstanding restaurants to your every taste and luxurious rooms to all your needs.
✉ **C/de Pau Claris 150, L'Eixample ☎ 93 487 62 62; fax 93 487 87 36** ⓔ **claris@derbyhotels .es; www.derbyhotels.es** Ⓜ **Passeig de Gracia** ✕ ♿ ♿ **excellent**

Hotel Condes de Barcelona (5, G2)

These dazzling digs occupy two spectacularly modernised 19th-century Modernista buildings. The pentagonal foyer is magnificent, the beds king-size and the baths big enough for a workout. If you stand

A room with a view, Your Majesty?

Martin Hughes

on your tippy-toes you can see La Pedrera from the rooftop terrace.
✉ **Pg de Gràcia 73-75, L'Eixample ☎ 93 488 22 00; fax 93 488 06 14** ⓔ **www.hotelcondes debarcelona.com** Ⓜ **Diagonal** ✕ ♿ **good**

Hotel Majèstic (5, H2)

A matter-of-fact eliteness pervades this beautiful hotel, which vies for the crown of flashiest in town. It comprises three splendid old buildings that were knocked into one (the family from one home now occupies the entire 9th floor). Rooms are tasteful, large and comfortable, while the two restaurants are very exclusive.
✉ **Pg de Gràcia 70, L'Eixample ☎ 93 488 17 17; fax 93 488 18 80** ⓔ **www.hotelmajestic .es** Ⓜ **Passeig de Gracia** ✕ ♿ ♿ **excellent**

Hotel Ritz (5, K4)

Founded in 1919 by Caesar Ritz, Barcelona's classic grand hotel offers more character and old-fashioned style than all the others put together. This hotel is a cornucopia of opulence from its imperial lobby to immense and luxuriant rooms with step-down Roman baths.
✉ **Gran Vía de les Corts Catalánes 668, L'Eixample ☎ 93 318 52 00; fax 93 318 01 48** ⓔ **www.ritzbcn.com** Ⓜ **Passeig de Gracia** ✕ ♿

Le Meridien Barcelona (4, C5)

Pink and plush, this is the best of the deluxe options on La Rambla. The top floor presidential suite is where the likes of Michael Jackson and Julio Iglesias used to rest their celebrity heads and all of its 212 rooms are elegantly furnished.
✉ **La Rambla 111 ☎ 93 318 62 00; fax 93 301 77 76** ⓔ **lemeridien@ meridienbarcelona.com** Ⓜ **Liceu** ✕

TOP END

Duques de Bergara

(4, A5) This hotel occupies a handsome early Modernista building (built in 1898) and has a handy location on a quiet street sandwiched between the old and new quarters. The foyer and stairways are original while the rest of the interior has been completely renovated. Rooms are pleasant and there's a pool big enough to work up a sweat in.

✉ C/de Bergara 11, L'Eixample ☎ 93 301 51 51; fax 93 317 31 79 e cataloni@hotels -catalonia.es; www .hoteles-catalonia.es Ⓜ Catalunya ✗ ⚲ ♿ excellent

Hotel Avenida Palace

(3, F5) If its minimalism you're after, skip to the next review because this 1952 establishment is a puzzle of different styles and patterns. A gentle calm eventually prevails and the hotel, popular with business folk, conveys an old-world atmosphere that

Night Life Versus Sleep

When you are not contributing to the racket yourself, raucous revellers, late-night garbage collection, overzealous sirens, church bells and barking dogs could all come between you and your zzzzzzs. Light sleepers should forsake the room with the wonderful view over the street and opt for the (often darker) one at the back.

belies its relative modernity. Service ranges depending on whose shift you're holidaying through.

✉ Gran Vía de les Corts Catalánes 605, L'Eixample ☎ 93 301 96 00; fax 93 318 12 34 e www.avenida palace.com Ⓜ Universitat

Hotel Colón (6, A4)

Housed behind a distinguished neo-classical facade on one of the city's most social spaces, this hotel offers stunning views across the cathedral. The rooms are tastefully furnished although doubles are two conjoined singles unless you specifically request a 'matrimonial'. The bar and restaurant are a bit stuffy and the staff should lighten up.

✉ Avda de la Catedral 7, Barri Gòtic ☎ 93 301 14 04; fax 93 317 29 15 e www.hotel colon.es Ⓜ Jaume I ✗ ⚲ ♿ good

Hotel Gran Via (3, E6)

This place oozes old-fashioned charm and much of its 19th-century interior remains intact. Guest rooms have been comfortably tweaked but the public areas, complete with antique furnishings, retain the grace of another age and there's a wonderful courtyard in which to relax after a long day.

✉ Gran Vía de les Corts Catalánes 642, L'Eixample ☎ 93 318 19 00; fax 93 318 99 97 e hgranvia@nn hoteles.es Ⓜ Passeig de Gracia

Hotel Inglaterra

(4, A4) This gleaming modern hotel lacks the sombre business-conference atmosphere of many others catering to professional travellers. Designed by local boy, Joan Pere, and decorated with Asian motifs and original art, it combines refined comforts with warm, efficient service and a central location.

✉ C/de Pelai 14, L'Eixample ☎ 93 505 11 00; fax 93 505 11 09 e hi@hotelingla terra.com; www.hotel majestic.es Ⓜ Universitat ✗ Café Zurich (p. 73) ♿ good

Hotel Oriente (4, F5)

A mouldering classic occupying part of a 17th-century monastery, the Oriente was established in 1842 as the city's first grand hotel. Rooms are spacious but spartan and the old place is fraying a little around the edges, but the wonderful public rooms make these some of the most atmospheric lodgings in Barcelona.

✉ La Rambla 45 ☎ 93 302 25 58; fax 93 412 38 19 e horiente@ husa.es; www.husa.es Ⓜ Drassanes or Liceu ✗

Hotel Rialto (4, E7)

Admirers of the great Catalan painter, Joan Miró, can stay in the house where he was born, which is now part of this otherwise unremarkable hotel. A generous buffet breakfast is served until 10am (not late enough) in an atmospheric vaulted basement.

✉ C/de Ferran 42, Barri Gòtic ☎ 93 318 52 12;

fax 93 318 53 12
Ⓜ Liceu ♿
✕ La Cerería (p. 76)

Hotel San Agustín
(4, E5) Travellers have been greeted with hearty *holas* at this place for well over a century, making it one of the oldest continually functioning hotels in the city. Rooms come with air-con, heating and satellite TV and the top floor rooms look out onto an expansive, peaceful square.
✉ Plaça de Sant Agustí 3, El Raval ☎ 93 318 16 58; fax 93 317 29 28 e www.hotelsa.com Ⓜ Liceu ✕ ♿ ♿ excellent

Hotel Suizo (6, D6)
There's a carefully cultivated old-world atmosphere within this 19th-century building, which includes a gorgeous *belle epoch* bar where guests converge each evening to swap their sightseeing stories.
The rooms are large and light, although the ones overlooking the nondescript plaça can be a bit noisy.
✉ Plaça de l'Àngel 12, Barri Gòtic ☎ 93 310 61 08; fax 93 310 40 81 Ⓜ Jaume I ✕ Buenas Migas (p. 74)

Rivoli Ramblas (4, C6)
For meticulous minimalism, luxurious colour schemes and an engagingly offbeat atmosphere, shelter at this modern renovation, where facilities include a gym with sauna and jacuzzi (a rarity in city hotels) as well as splendid views of the old city from the roof-terrace and a dangerously tempting cocktail bar.
✉ La Rambla 128 ☎ 93 302 66 43, reservations 93 412 09 88; fax 93 317 50 53 e rivoli@mssl.es; www.rivolihotels.com Ⓜ Catalunya or Liceu ✕

Martin Hughes

Handle a decent room?

MID-RANGE

Barcelona House Hotel (4, G6)
Big, gay and endearingly kooky, this hotel has 70 (mostly) spacious rooms, each decked out in a different shade of kitsch. Expect warm colours, retro features and baths big enough for company. Continental breakfasts are served until 11am and there's a passageway to the popular Café Royale (p. 89) so you can avoid the queues.
✉ Ptge dels Escudellers 19, Barri Gòtic ☎ 93 301 82 95 e hbhouse@interplanet.es Ⓜ Drassanes ✕ Taxidermista (p. 79)

Hostal Orleans
(4, F11) On the edge of the old quarters, this affable accommodation comprises large rooms (many en suite), a cosy and tranquil living room, and an owner whose warm welcome is ample compensation for the three flights of stairs you must climb. There's no safe available though.
✉ Avda del Marques de l'Argentina 13, La Ribera ☎ 93 319 73 82; fax 93 319 22 19 Ⓜ Barceloneta ✕ Salero (p. 82)

Breakfast Included
Many hotels include breakfast in their rates but there's usually precious little value added. What constitutes breakfast in some places could be a miserable cold bun, which really isn't worth dragging yourself out of bed for. And it's usually served too early, which doesn't fit in with Barcelona's late social hours. All up, don't be swayed by the 'breakfast included' deal because it will usually be more rewarding to venture to a nearby cafe.

Hostal San Remo

(5, K5) You'll get the most jovial welcome at this cute hostal, which has pleasant and comfortable rooms with air-con, en suite and double-glazed windows. Some have sunny balconies but none have double beds. Meenie, the fluffy white mutt, does room visits upon request and Rosa, the owner, is an absolute darling.

✉ **C/d'Ausiàs Marc 19, L'Eixample**
☎ **93 302 19 89; fax 93 301 07 74**
Ⓜ **Urquinaona**

Hotel California (4, F6)

One of the few hotels to openly welcome gay guests, this place has an unbeatable location in the heart of Barri Gòtic. Some of the rooms (all en suite) are a little grim but the multi-lingual reception opens 24hrs.

✉ **C/d'En Rauric 14, Barri Gòtic** ☎ **93 317 77 66** Ⓜ **Liceu**
✕ **Can Culleretes (p. 74)**

Hotel Continental

(4, B6) If you're looking forward to getting stuck into George Orwell's *Homage to Catalonia*, where better than the place where the author recovered from a bullet wound? Space is scarce in most of the rooms but some have semi-circular balconies with wonderful views over the life of La Rambla.

✉ **La Rambla 138**
☎ **93 301 25 70; fax 93 302 73 60** ⓔ **www .hotelcontinental.com**
Ⓜ **Catalunya** ✕ **Café Zurich (p. 73)**

Hotel España (4, F5)

If Modernisme means more to you than comfort, then head to this landmark hotel, the lower floors of which were designed by Domènech i Montaner, the father of the movement, and decorated by the most celebrated artists and artisans of the era. The dining rooms are magnificent but the guest rooms are functional and drab.

✉ **C/de Sant Pau 9-11, El Raval** ☎ **93 318 17 58; fax 93 317 11 34**
ⓔ **hotelespanya@ tresnet.com** Ⓜ **Liceu** ✕

Hotel Internacional

(4, E6) If you're a football fan over for a match, you're probably already booked in here and looking forward to draping your colours over its mid-La Rambla balcony. You'll be happy to know that while the rooms are only adequate, there's a pleasant and relaxed dining room and a lively little bar.

✉ **La Rambla 78-80**
☎ **93 302 25 66; fax 93 317 61 90**
ⓔ **www.husa.es**
Ⓜ **Liceu** ✕ **Can Culleretes (p. 74)**

Hotel Mesón de Castilla (4, B4)

This hotel feels more country than city, thanks to its warm staff and soothing atmosphere. The rooms are gracefully furnished, the public rooms are congenial

Welcome to the Hotel Internacional

Martin Hughes

and bear a wealth of Modernista features, and the interior patio is a delightful place to start the day by tucking into a hearty buffet breakfast.

✉ C/de Valldon Zella 5, El Raval ☎ 93 318 21 82; fax 93 412 40 20

e hmesoncastilla@ teleline.es

Ⓜ Universitat ✕ Café Zurich (p. 73)

Hotel Paseo de Gracia (5, F2)

If you'd rather spend your lolly browsing boutiques than on your lodgings, this pleasant hotel is in the heart of l'Eixample and, quite literally, in amongst some irresistible shops. Rooms are fine and have terrific views down on to the street that Gaudi made famous.

✉ Pg de Gracia 102,
L'Eixample ☎ 93 215 58 24; fax 93 215 06 03

Ⓜ Diagonal ✕ Mauri Patisserie (p. 84)

Hotel Peninsular (4, F5)

Once part of a convent, this wonderful little hotel on the fringe of the Barri Xinès has clean, spacious and economic rooms set along curved balconies overlooking a vast, plant-lined atrium. They only have one star but, as the friendly brothers who run it like to say, it's the biggest one.

✉ C/de Sant Pau 34,
Raval ☎ 93 302 31 38; fax 93 412 36 99

Ⓜ Liceu ✕ Rita Blue (p. 77)

Hotel Triunfo (4, D12)

Standing proudly on a dilapidated stretch of Pg de Picasso between lively El Borne and Parc de la
Ciutadella, this simple hotel has a great location if you want to party by night and loll in a park by day. Rooms are modest.

✉ Pg de Picasso 22,
La Ribera ☎ 93 315 08 60; fax 93 315 08 60

Ⓜ Barceloneta
✕ Commerç 24 (p. 81)

Pension Francia (4, F11)

The homely smell of laundry pervades this quaint little hostal close to shore, park and nightlife of El Borne. It's run by two lively old sisters who do their best to accommodate guests in between dashing to answer radio quizzes. The best rooms are on the second floor.

✉ C/de Rera Palau 4 pral, La Ribera
☎ 93 319 03 76

Ⓜ Barceloneta
✕ La Tinaja (p. 82)

BUDGET

Casa Huéspedes Mari-Luz (4, F7)

This is a convivial little spot in a quiet and atmospheric part of the Barri Gòtic. Bright and sunny rooms, complete with wooden beams, are well maintained and the hostess is obliging and chirpy. Only a few of the rooms have showers, while others can accommodate groups at a squeeze.

✉ C/del Palau 4, Barri Gòtic ☎ 93 317 34 63

Ⓜ Jaume I ✕ Café Just (p. 74)

Hostal Galerias Maldà (4, D6)

This family-run hostal is part of a rambling house inside Barcelona's first arcade. Some of its 21
rooms are big enough to swing several cats in but none are en suite. It feels like a home from home but, with your own door key, you're welcome to treat this place like a hotel.

✉ C/del Pi 5, Barri Gòtic ☎ 93 317 30 02

Ⓜ Liceu ✕ Menage a Trois (p. 77)

Hostal Layetana (6, B6)

Virtually leaning against the ancient Roman wall, this third floor hotel is comfortably basic. The superb antique lift will reignite your childhood fascination for such things but press 'Hs' instead of '3'. Traffic noise and cathedral bells are the only downside.

✉ Plaça de Ramon
Berenguer el Gran, Barri Gòtic
☎ 93 319 20 12; fax 93 319 20 12

Ⓜ Jaume 1
✕ Café d'Estiu (p. 74)

Hostal Oliva (5, J3)

A picturesque antique lift wheezes its way up to this 4th-floor hostel, a terrific cheapie in Barcelona's most expensive neighbourhood. Some of the singles are barely big enough to fit a bed but the doubles are large, light and airy, and several have fabulous views over Barcelona's grandest street.

✉ Pg de Gràcia 32
☎ 93 488 01 62; fax 93 488 17 89

Ⓜ Passeig de Gracia

Child's Play

Apart from the top-end places, which cater to every whim, Barcelona's hotels aren't known for being family friendly. Many of them are located up long flights of stairs and sound-proofing is often a problem – adding that extra challenge to putting youngsters to sleep at night (and your kids' rise-and-shine in the mornings might cause the clubbers next door pain). Luckily there are a few places that recognise kids as travellers too. Look for the child-friendly icon ♿.

Hostal Parisien (4, D6)

Sociable and central, this popular place hums all day with music and the comings and goings of a young crowd. Those with an aversion to birds should steer clear because a very large (and very uncaged) parrot named Frederico occupies the foyer. Rooms range from basic dorms to comfortably compact en suite doubles.

✉ La Rambla 114
☎ 93 301 62 83;
fax 93 301 62 83
Ⓜ Liceu ✕ Menage a Trois (p. 77)

Hostal-Residencia Rembrandt (4, D6)

Another outrageously popular budget option, the choice of the spic-and-span rooms (all en suite) here come with balconies where you can watch the bustle of Barri Gòtic's busiest pedestrian street. There's also a nice communal patio.

✉ C/de la Portaferrissa 23, Barri Gòtic
☎ /fax 93 318 10 11
Ⓜ Liceu ✕ Menage a Trois (p. 77)

Hotel Jardi Map (4, D6)

You should maybe start thinking about booking this place for your *next* visit as the double rooms overlooking the sociable and traffic-free plaça are the most sought after in the city. Rooms at the back are cheaper and dingier.

✉ Plaça de Sant Josep Oriol 1, Barri Gòtic
☎ 93 301 59 00;
fax 93 318 36 64
Ⓜ Liceu ✕ Menage a Trois (p. 77)

Hotel Roma Reial

(4, F6) Located in a corner of the seducingly seedy Plaça Reial, this hugely popular budget hotel has a grand foyer that will make you think you've got the address wrong. The serviceable rooms, all with private facilities, aren't half bad either and some provide balconied vantage points for enjoying the square.

✉ **Plaça Reial 11, Barri Gòtic** ☎ 93 302 03 66;
fax 93 301 18 39
Ⓜ Liceu
✕ Taxidermista (p. 79)

Residencia Windsor

(5, G1) This is a good inexpensive option on one of the city's loveliest ramblas. Singles can be a little small and dark but the doubles are more than adequate, particularly those with views over the street. Quaint Victorianesque furnishings and mild-mannered staff give it a pleasant and homely vibe.

✉ **Rambla de Catalunya 84, L'Eixample**
☎ 93 215 11 98
Ⓜ Diagonal ✕ Mauri Patisserie (p. 84)

Rey don Jaime I

(6, E4) Perfect if you want to straddle the nightlife of Barri Gòtic and La Ribera, this is a good value cheapo with a feint touch of class in its tiny gilt lobby. Basic rooms all come with balconies and bathrooms but the ones at the front are noisy even by Barcelona's standards.

✉ **C/de Jaume I, Barri Gòtic** ☎ 93 310 62 08
🅴 r.d.Jaime@atrium hotels.com
Ⓜ Jaume I ✕ Buenas Migas (p. 74)

Stay near the clowns in Barri Gòtic.

Martin Hughes

facts for the visitor

Martin Hughes

The only way is down... to the metro.

ARRIVAL & DEPARTURE

Barcelona is easily accessible by air from anywhere in Europe and North America. Regular rail and bus links, and a smooth super highway, connect it with France and the rest of Europe while there are plenty of air and land connections to destinations all over Spain.

Air

Aeroport del Prat, Barcelona's airport, lies 12km southwest of the city and contains three terminals: 'A' handles non-EU arrivals and non-Spanish airlines; 'B' handles EU arrivals, Spanish airlines and some of the overspill from A; and 'C' handles the Barcelona-Madrid shuttle. There are tourist offices and facilities at terminals A and B.

Left Luggage

The *consigna* (left luggage) office is on the ground floor at the end of terminal B and charges €4 per item per day.

Information

For flight and general information, call ☎ 93 298 38 38 and listen carefully for the option to choose English.

Airport Access

Train It's about 20mins to the city by train, which connects the airport and the city stations of Estació Sants, Plaça Catalunya, Arc de Triomf and Clot-Aragò (all of which are, conveniently, also metro stations). A single ticket costs €2.30 and trains leave the airport at 13 and 43 minutes past the hour between 6.13am and 10.43pm. Trains from Plaça Catalunya to the airport leave at 8 and 38 minutes past the hour between 5.38am and 10.08pm.

Metro A new metro line should connect the city and the airport by 2004.

Aerobùs This bus service runs from the airport to Plaça de Catalunya via Estació Sants every 15 minutes from 6am to midnight (from 6.30am weekends and holidays). Departures from Plaça de Catalunya are from 5.30am to 11.15pm Monday to Friday and from 6am to 11.20pm on weekends and holidays. The trip takes just over half an hour and costs €3 (pay onboard).

Taxi The queues outside the airport move pretty quickly and the half hour journey to the city centre costs around €15.

Train

Virtually all long-distance trains run by Spanish state railways, RENFE, use Estació Sants (3, G1), which also has a metro station (Sants Estació). Trains run to most Spanish cities and there is a mind-boggling array of fare options. The quickest service to Madrid, the Talgo, costs €39.60 for a single and takes 6½hrs. For info on all RENFE services, call ☎ 902 24 02 02 (24hrs) or visit ⓔ www.renfe.es.

The best train to and from Paris is the *trenhotel* sleeper. It leaves in the evenings, takes 12hrs and costs €102. Call ☎ 93 490 11 22 for information. A direct Talgo service connects Montpellier with Barcelona (€38.40, 4½hrs). Barcelona is in the process of being linked to the French TGV network.

Bus

The main intercity bus station is Estació del Nord (3, E8; ☎ 93 265 65 08). A few long-distance international services (and buses to Montserrat use Estació d'Autobusos de Sants (3, G1) beside Estació Sants.

The main international services are run by Eurolines/Julià Via (☎ 93 490 40 00) from Estació d'Autobusos de Sants and by Eurolines/Linebùs (☎ 93 265 07 00) from Estació del Nord (3, E8).

Travel Documents

Passport

Spain is party to the Schengen agreement and there is usually no passport control for arrivals from within the EU although you are obliged to carry your passport or a national ID card.

Visa

Visas are not required by citizens of the EU, USA, Canada, Australia, New Zealand, Israel, Japan and Switzerland for tourist visits of up to three months. If you are a citizen of a country not listed here, check with your Spanish consulate before you travel as you may need a specific visa. If you intend to stay for more than three months you must apply for a resident's card.

Customs & Duty Free

If you've paid the duty, you are allowed to bring in the equivalent of 800 cigarettes, 10L of spirits, 90L of wine and 110L of beer. Check with your home country on what you're allowed to bring back. Arrivals from outside the EU are allowed to bring in 200 cigarettes, 50 cigars or 250g of tobacco, 1L of spirits and 2L of wine duty free.

Departure Tax

This is factored into the price of your ticket so you won't have any last minute flapping about when you've spent all your euros.

GETTING AROUND

Barcelona has a user-friendly public transport system. The metro stops close to most places of interest (although you will normally have to walk to places deep in the old quarters) and is complemented by the suburban rail system FGC and an extensive network of bus routes.

Although there are night buses, the main public transport system finishes around 1am to 2am on weekends, which is out of sync with Barcelona's social habits, and it can be a nightmare trying to get a cab. You can get a map of bus and metro routes at the main tourist office on Plaça Catalunya (4, A7).

Travel Passes

Targetas are integrated multiple-trip tickets that will save you time and money and are sold at most metro stations. T-10 (€5.35) gives you 10 trips on metro, buses and FGC trains. T-Dia (€4) gives you unlimited travel for one day, T-50/30 (€22.20) allows you 50 trips within 30 days, and so on. You can also get an all-in-one targeta for the Aerobùs, metro and buses valid for three (€13.20) or five (€16.80) days.

Metro

The metro has five numbered and colour-coded lines, which are efficient and easy to use (the stations get a little more basic the further you stray from the tourist areas). When interchanging, the direction and destination of the lines are indicated in green. Single tickets, good for one journey no matter how many changes you have to make, cost €0.90. The metro operates from 5am to 11pm Monday to Thursday, until 2am Friday and Saturday (and the day before public holidays) and has a reduced service from 6am to midnight on Sunday.

FGC

This suburban network will come in handy for trips to scattered attractions such as Tibidabo and Pedralbes from Plaça Catalunya. It operates on the same schedule as the metro and a single ticket costs the same (€0.90).

Bus

Most buses run between 6am and 10.30pm Monday to Thursday and until 2am Friday, Saturday and the days before holidays. After 2am a reduced schedule of more expensive yellow *nitbusos* (night buses) operates until 4am. Many pass through Plaça Catalunya. You enter at the front and exit through the middle doors. Only single tickets (€0.90) can be bought on board and *targetas* are validated in a machine behind the driver.

Taxi

Barcelona's black-and-yellow cabs are reasonably priced and can be hailed when a green light on the roof shows that they are *libre* (free). The flagfall is €1.80 for the first 2km, and then €0.66 per additional kilometre from 6am to 10pm Monday to Friday (about 20% higher at all other times). You are also charged €0.90 per item of luggage that must go in

the boot and it's an additional €1.80 for trips to and from the airport. On weekend nights especially you'll have trouble getting a cab if your journey doesn't appeal to the driver.

Car & Motorcycle

Frankly, with the combination of a complex one-way system, impatient drivers, the possibility of theft and slim hopes of ever finding a parking space, you'd be better off using the public transport than driving your own vehicle. If you do want to drive, your licence from home will usually suffice. Bear in mind that the speed limits aren't always adhered to and when oncoming drivers flash their lights it usually means 'I ain't slowing down'. It's also common to race through amber lights so be careful before braking at these or you might get rear-ended.

If you've got the nerve and the experience, scooters are the mode en vogue and are obviously much easier to park.

Parking

Apart from August, when most of the locals have nicked off on their holidays, looking for parking is a stress. As a general guide: red markings mean not on your life, blue mean pay and display, and yellow mean you can park for up to half an hour if you're loading and unloading. Tickets and tows are common in the yellow zones, especially during working hours Monday to Saturday. Use the municipal car parks if you've got foreign plates as these tend to be safer.

Rental

Car hire is relatively expensive in Barcelona and generally not worth it unless you're planning more than a couple of day trips. Local firms such as Julià Car (☎ 93 402 69 00) and Vanguard (☎ 93 439 38 80) are generally cheaper than the big international names, who you'll find at the airport and Estació Sants. A small car with unlimited kilometres will cost around €108 for three days or €210 for a week, plus tax and insurance. You will have to put down a hefty bond by way of cash or credit card.

There are quite a few scooter-hire companies but you usually need to book in advance for their limited range, which can cost anything from €24 to €60 per day. Start with Moto Scooter (☎ 93 215 93 79) or Vanguard (☎ 93 439 38 80), who will give you other places to try if they can't accommodate you.

Motoring Organisations

The Real Automòvil Club de España (RACE; ☎ 900 11 22 22) is usually for members only but check with your home motoring organisation, which might have reciprocal rights with it.

PRACTICAL INFORMATION

Climate & When to Go

Barcelona's Mediterranean climate brings cool winters and hot summers. In July and much of August, the heat and humidity can be torrid with temperatures sometimes nudging 37°C. From January to March, temperatures can plummet to a crisp 5°C. Late April and May are pleasant times to visit, as are September and early October if you're lucky enough to avoid the late summer thunderstorms that see pavement tables being dragged indoors. During the summer you can expect lots of blue sky but also the occasional downpour.

The combination of tourists and business travellers visiting the city means that hotels are busy for most of the year and there's really no such thing as an off-season. June and September are best for festivals while the city is transformed in August when much of the population holidays elsewhere and many places are closed.

Tourist Information

Tourist Information Abroad

The Oficina Española de Turismo has many international offices that supply information about travelling to Spain.

Canada
  2 Bloor St West, 34th floor, Toronto M4W 3E2 (☎ 416-961 3131; [e] toronto@ tourspain.es, www.tourspain.toronto.on.ca)

France
  43 rue Decamps, 75784 Paris, Cedex 16 (☎ 01 45 03 82 57; fax 01 45 03 82 51; [e] paris@tourspain.es, www.espagne .infotourisme.com)

Japan
  Daini Toranomon Denki Bldg 4f, 3-1-10 Toranomon, Minato-Ku (☎ 03-34 32 61 41; [e] tokio@tourspain.es)

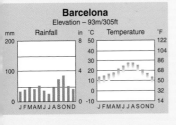

Barcelona
Elevation – 93m/305ft

mm	Rainfall	in	°C	Temperature	°F
200		8	50		122
			40		104
			30		86
100		4	20		68
			10		50
			0		32
0	J F M A M J J A S O N D	0	-10	J F M A M J J A S O N D	14

UK

22-23 Manchester Square, London W1M 5AP (☎ 020-7486 8077 or 0906 364 0630 for brochure request; e londres@ tourspain.es, www.tourspain.co.uk)

USA

666 Fifth Ave, 35th floor, New York, NY 10103 (☎ 212-265 8822; e oetny@ tourspain.es, www.okspain.org); there are also branches in Chicago, Los Angeles and Miami

Local Tourist Information

The Oficina d'Informació de Turisme de Barcelona (4, A7; Plaça de Catalunya 17-S; ☎ 906 30 12 82 from within Spain or 93 304 34 21 from abroad) provides excellent information on the city and can help book accommodation if you're in a jam. However, it can get very crowded. It opens 9am to 9pm and has branches in the city council building on Plaça Sant Jaume (6, E3), at Estació Sants (3, G1) and at La Sagrada Família (3, C6) during the summer. Information officers in red jackets also roam the Barri Gòtic in summer, answering queries in a very impressive variety of languages.

The excellent Palau Robert at Pg de Gràcia 107 (5, F1; ☎ 93 238 40 00) specialises in information on the whole of Catalunya.

Consulates

Australia

9th floor, Gran Via de Carles III 98 (2, F4; ☎ 93 330 94 96)

Canada

Pg de Gràcia 77 (5, G2; ☎ 93 215 07 04)

Ireland

Gran Via de Carles III (2, F4; ☎ 93 491 50 21)

Japan

Avda Diagonal 662-664 (2, E4; ☎ 93 280 34 33)

New Zealand

Travesssera de Gràcia 64 (3, D3; ☎ 93 209 03 99)

UK

Avda Diagonal 477 (3, E2; ☎ 93 419 90 44)

USA

Pg de la Reina Elisenda de Montcada 23-25 (2, D3; ☎ 93 280 02 95)

Money

Currency

The euro was introduced to Spain on 1 January 2002 and the peseta withdrawn on 1 March. There are seven euro notes (5, 10, 20, 50, 100, 200 and 500) in different colours and sizes, and eight euro coins (one, two, five, 10, 20 and 50 cents and 1 and 2 euros).

This book was researched during the transition period and some prices may undergo further change as the euro comes into use.

Travellers Cheques

Travellers cheques are useful because they can be replaced if lost or stolen. American Express and Thomas Cook are widely accepted brands. You will need your passport when cashing cheques. Banks will generally offer better rates but *cambio* (exchange) offices open longer and are quicker.

Credit Cards

Apart from at budget establishments, you can pay with plastic in most places. Check with your bank about charges before you leave home. Very few traders check signatures here so if you lose your card, you can get fleeced very quickly. In case of emergency call:

American Express	☎ 91 572 03 03
Diners Club	☎ 91 547 40 00
MasterCard	☎ 900 97 12 31
Visa	☎ 900 97 44 45

ATMs

Telebancos (ATMs) can be found on most streets and you can use them as long as you're connected to the Cirrus and/or Maestro networks. They usually work out cheaper than exchanging travellers cheques.

Tipping

Restaurants are required by law to include service charges in their menu prices so tipping is a matter of personal choice. Most people leave some small change if they're satisfied (5% is usually plenty). It's common to leave small change at bar and cafe tables. Hotel porters won't harass you if you tip them €1.

Discounts

Concessions (up to 50%) are available for youth and students, as well as seniors (with the appropriate identification) at most attractions and on some public transport. It's worth flashing your ID wherever you go because some places don't shout about their concessions but grant them nonetheless.

Student & Youth Cards

The most widely accepted forms of student identification are the International Student Identity Card (ISIC) or the Carnet Joven Europeo (Euro<26 card).

Travel Insurance

A policy covering theft, loss, medical expenses and compensation for cancellation or delays in your travel arrangements is highly recommended. If items are lost or stolen, make sure you get a police report straight away – otherwise your insurer might not pay up.

Opening Hours

Once you adjust to Barcelona's schedule, you'll find that opening hours are pretty consistent across business type.

Shops generally open between 9am and 10am Monday to Saturday and close for lunch by 2pm. They reopen around 4.30pm and carry on until 8pm or 9pm. Allow for a lie-in and a more leisurely lunch on Saturday. Virtually all shops close on Sunday. Traders on the main tourist thoroughfares often stay open throughout the day.

Opening times for tourist sites vary. Museums tend to keep the same hours as shops (although usually without the break for lunch) but have shorter schedules in winter. Virtually all museums, and many other attractions, close on Monday.

Normal banking hours are 8.30am to 2pm Monday to Friday and 8.30am to 1pm Saturday. Most shut on public holidays but this can vary so check.

Public Holidays

Jan 1	New Year's Day
Jan 6	Three Kings' Day
Mar/Apr	Good Friday
Mar/Apr	Easter Monday
May 1	Labour Day
May/Jun	Whit Monday
June 24	Feast of St John
Aug 15	Feast of the Assumption
Sep 11	Catalan National Day
Sep 24	Barcelona Day
Oct 12	Spanish National Day
Nov 1	All Saints Day
Dec 8	Feast of the Immaculate Conception
Dec 25	Christmas Day
Dec 26	St Stephen's Day

Time

Spanish Standard Time is one hour ahead of GMT/UTC during winter and two hours ahead during the daylight-saving period (from the last Sunday in March to the last Sunday in October). At noon in Barcelona it's:

6am in New York
3am in Los Angeles
11am in London
1pm in Johannesburg
11pm in Auckland
9pm in Sydney

Electricity

The electric current is 220V, 50Hz and plugs have two round pins, as in the rest of continental Europe. Adapters are best bought at home but can also be purchased at FNAC and other shops in Barcelona. Several countries outside Europe (such as the USA and Canada) have 60Hz, which means that appliances with electric motors (such as some CD and tape players) from those countries may perform poorly. It is always safest to use a transformer.

Weights & Measures

Spain uses the metric system and, like the rest of continental Europe, Spaniards indicate decimals with commas and thousands with points. See the conversion table (p.122) for more details.

Post

Stamps are sold at most *estancs* (tobacconist shops with 'Tabacs' in yellow letters on a maroon background) as well as at Correus i Telègrafs/Correos y Telégrafos (post offices). The main post office is on Plaça d'Antoni López (4, G9; ☎ 902 19 71 97; Mon-Sat 8am-9.30pm) and offers a poste restante service (windows 7 and 8). Another useful post office is just off Pg de Gràcia at Carrer d'Aragó 282 (5, H3; Mon-Fri

8.30am-8.30pm, Sat 9.30am-1pm). Other district offices tend to open from 8am to 2pm Monday to Friday .

Postal Rates

A standard letter or postcard costs €0.45 to anywhere else in Europe, €0.70 to North America and €1.11 to Australasia and Asia.

Telephone

The ubiquitous blue payphones are easy to use for international and domestic calls. They accept coins, phone cards and sometimes credit cards. A three-minute local call from a street payphone costs around €0.15, more from public phones in bars etc. Cheap call centres are springing up across town, especially in areas such as El Raval with large migrant communities, but know what is and isn't a good rate before dialling.

International calls are cheaper from 8pm to 8am on weekdays and all weekend.

Phonecards

Tarjetas telefónicas (phonecards) are sold at post offices, estancs and many newsstands.

Lonely Planet's eKno Communication Card, specifically aimed at travellers, provides competitive international calls (avoid using it for local calls), messaging services and free email. For more information, visit the eKno Web site at e www.ekno.lonelyplanet.com.

Mobile Phones

Spain uses the GSM cellular phone system, compatible with phones sold in just about everywhere except the USA and Japan. To use the network, you must first set up a global roaming service with your service provider before you leave home.

Country & City Codes

Note that area codes are an integral part of all telephone numbers in Spain, even if you are calling within a single zone. So any number you are calling in Barcelona will start with ☎ 93 regardless of whether you are in Barcelona or in another part of Spain.

Spain	☎ 34
Barcelona	☎ 93

Useful Numbers

Local Directory Enquiries	☎ 1003
International Directory Enquiries	☎ 025
Local Operator	☎ 1009
International Operator Europe/North Africa	☎ 1008
International Operator Rest of the World	☎ 1005
International Collect Call	☎ 900 (+ code for the country you are calling)
Time	☎ 093
Weather	☎ 906 365 365

International Direct Dial Codes

The access code for international calls is ☎ 00, which will give you a new dialling tone.

Australia	☎ 61
Canada	☎ 1
Japan	☎ 81
New Zealand	☎ 64
South Africa	☎ 27
UK	☎ 44
USA	☎ 1

Digital Resources

If you're travelling with your computer, make sure you have a universal AC adapter and a plug adapter. Spanish phone sockets have mostly been standardised to the US RJ-11 type. For more information on travelling with a portable computer, see [e] www.teleadapt.com or www.warrior.com.

Internet Service Providers

Major Internet service providers (ISPs) such as AOL ([e] www.aol.com) and CompuServe ([e] www.compuserve.com), as well as AT&T Business Internet Services ([e] www.attbusiness.net) have dial-in nodes throughout Europe, including in the major Spanish cities. It's best to download a list of the dial-in numbers before you leave home.

Internet Cafes

Try one of the following cybercafes if you're in need of an email fix:

easyEverything
Ronda Universitat 35, L'Eixample (4, A5; ☎ 93 412 10 58; [e] www.easyeverything.com; 24hrs; different rates depending on demand); also at La Rambla 31

Over the Game
C/de la Fusina 7, El Borne (4, E11; ☎ 93 268 10 80 [e] www.overthegame.es; 10am-1am; €1.80 per 30mins)

El Café de Internet
Gran Vía de les Corts Catalánes 656, L'Eixample (3, E6; ☎ 93 412 19 15; [e] cafe@cafeinternet.es; Mon-Sat 10am-10pm; €1.50 per 30mins)

Bc-net
C/Barra de Ferro 3, La Ribera; (4, E9; ☎ 93 268 15 07; [e] www.bcnetcafe.com; 10am-1am; €1.80 per 30mins)

Idea
Plaça Comercial 2, El Borne (4, E11; ☎ 93 268 87 87; [e] www.ideaborn.com; Mon-Fri 9am-midnight, Sat 10.30am-2am, Sun 10.30am-midnight; €1.80 per 30mins)

Useful Sites

The Lonely Planet Web site ([e] www.lonelyplanet.com) offers a speedy link to many Barcelona Web sites. Others to try include:

Barcelona City Council
[e] www.bcn.es

Barcelona On Line
[e] www.deinfo.es/barcelona-on-line

Generalitat de Catalunya
e www.gencat.es

Infobarn
e www.barcelonaturisme.com

Internet Cafe Guide
e www.netcafeguide.com

RENFE
e www.renfe.es

All About Spain
e www.red2000.com

CitySync

CitySync Barcelona, Lonely Planet's digital guide for Palm OS handheld devices, allows quick searches, sorting and bookmarking of hundreds of Barcelona's attractions, clubs, hotels, restaurants and more, all pinpointed on scrollable street maps. Purchase or demo CitySync Barcelona at **e** www.citysync.com.

Doing Business

All the deluxe and top-end hotels have business facilities including conference rooms, secretarial services, fax and photocopying services, use of computers, private office space etc. If they don't provide translation services, they will know somebody who can.

Established to assist foreigners holding conference or events in the city, the Barcelona Convention Bureau (3, H2; C/de Tarragona 149, L'Eixample; ☎ 93 423 18 00) is a good place to start for general information and guidance. It opens 9am to 2.30pm and 4pm to 6pm Monday to Friday.

Newspapers & Magazines

The Castilian *La Vanguardia* has been Barcelona's leading daily for donkey's years although *El Periódico*, published in Castilian and Catalan, has recently been outselling it. But the left-leaning national *El País* is Spain's best while *El Mundo* prides itself on uncovering political scandals. *Avui* is the Catalan nationalist daily and *Marca* is devoted exclusively to sport.

International papers are stocked at most newsstands. In various bars you'll find the free English-language monthly *Barcelona Metropolitan*, which is aimed at expats and most useful for its ads. *Business Barcelona* (€1.20) is a monthly English-language business paper that is often full of insightful articles on the city's commercial life. The style and fashion quarterly, *b-guided*, is an excellent (if advertising driven) guide to happening bars, restaurants, shops and the rest and is sold in acceptably cool venues.

Radio

BBC World Service broadcasts on a variety of frequencies (648kHz, 9410kHz and 12,095kHz) depending on the time of day. Likewise, search for Voice of America on 9700kHz, 9760kHz and 15,205kHz. The Spanish national network Radio Nacional de España (RNE) has several stations, of which RNE 1 (738AM, 88.3FM) is the one specialising in general interest and current affairs programmes. Among the most listened to rock and pop stations are 40 Principales (93.9FM), Onda Cero (89.1FM) and Cadena 100 (100FM). If you want to hear Catalan on the radio, tune into Catalunya Ràdio (102.8FM) or Ràdio Espanya Catalunya (94.9FM).

TV

Most TVs receive seven channels (eight if you're lucky). TVE1 and TVE2 are state-run and broadcast a combination of pro-government news and good arts programmes and movies. Antena 3, Tele 5 and Canal Plus are all commercial channels and broadcast the usual diet of mainstream fodder with some late-night sauciness. TV3 is the Catalunya regional government channel with mainstream broadcasts that are entirely in Catalan. Canal 33, also in Catalan, specialises in sports and documentaries while the now-you-see-it-now-you-don't BTV is run by the city council and has a popular nightly news bulletin at 9pm as well as lots of local interest programming. Many homes, and some hotels, also have satellite.

Photography & Video

Most main brands of film are widely available and processing is fast and efficient. A roll of print film (36 exposures, ISO 100) costs around €3.60 for overnight service while slide (diapositiva) transparencies will cost you around €4.50.

Apri Foto Video at La Rambla 38-40 (4, G6; ☎ 93 301 74 04) may be able to help you with simple repairs but if you've got a major problem your best bet is to look up a specialist dealing in your make of equipment in the telephone directory.

Spain uses the PAL video system, which is not compatible with other standards unless converted.

Health

There are no specific health risks in Barcelona as health and hygiene standards are generally pretty good and tap water is drinkable. The only problems you're likely to encounter are sunburn, dehydration and/or mild and initial gut problems if you're not used to eating a lot of olive oil. Pharmacists are generally fairly sympathetic when it comes to dispensing most medicines without a prescription.

While AIDS has been on the decrease in recent years, the HIV virus continues to spread among diverse groups. Like anywhere else, practise the usual precautions; condoms are available in pharmacies and supermarkets.

Insurance & Medical Treatment

EU residents are covered for emergency medical treatment through Spain's public health service as long as they supply (within four days) an E111 form from their national health body. Non-EU citizens should check with their policies at home to see if they are covered for any mishaps in Spain. Regardless, travel insurance is advisable to cover any medical treatment you may need while in Barcelona.

Medical Services

In an emergency, head straight to the urgències (casualty ward). For an ambulance, call ☎ 061 or 93 329 97 01 or 93 300 20 20. Hospitals with 24hr accident and emergency departments include:

Hospital de la Creu Roja
C/del Dos de Maig 301 (3, A7; ☎ 93 300 20 20)

Hospital de la Santa Creu i de Sant Pau
C/de Sant Antoni Maria Claret 167 (3, A6; ☎ 93 291 90 00)

Hospital Clinic i Provincial
C/de Villaroel 170 (3, E3; ☎ 93 227 54 00)

Dental Services

Dental services (inevitably costly) are not covered by reciprocal rights within the EU, another good reason to get travel insurance. If you require emergency treatment, head to the Centre Odontològic at C/Calàbria 251 (3, F2; ☎ 93 439 45 00; Mon-Fri 9am-9pm, Sat 9am-2pm, shorter hours in Aug).

Pharmacies

The following pharmacies are open 24hrs:

Farmàcia Clapés
  La Rambla 98 (4, D6; ☎ 93 301 28 43)

Farmàcia Alvarez
  Pg de Gràcia 26, L'Eixample (5, J3; ☎ 93 302 11 24)

Toilets

Public lavs aren't common but wandering into bars and cafes to use their conveniences is acceptable – the locals do it all the time. You might want to carry a wad of your own loo paper.

Safety Concerns

Pick pocketing and theft are the problems most likely to rain on your holiday parade. Barcelona has been ranked Europe's worst city for credit card theft, petty crime is endemic and a string of experienced guidebook writers are among the list of hapless victims.

Keep only a limited amount of cash on you, and the bulk of your money in replaceable forms such as travellers cheques or plastic. Use your hotel safe. Money or valuables that you need to take out with you should be in a shoulder wallet or concealed money belt. If you wear an external money belt, you might as well paint a big target sign on your back. Men should carry their swag in their front pockets only and women should wear bags across their bodies and never hanging from the shoulder. If you're carrying a daypack, even if it's on your back the whole time, don't leave valuables in any accessible pockets. Be particularly alert on the metro, in heavily touristed parts of town such as La Rambla and Barri Gòtic and on the beaches in summer. Also, the port side of El Raval – what's left of

the notorious Barrio Xines – is not the place to play the clueless tourist. In general, be wary of anybody who goes out of their way to be just that little bit too helpful as scams are on the increase.

Never leave anything visible in your car and preferably leave nothing at all. Don't get a hire car that has any marking identifying it as such and beware that if you have foreign plates you're going to be even more vulnerable.

Honestly, you may think you're sharp as a tack but these guys are masterful crooks and it's well worth doubling the level of your own personal security to avoid holiday hardship.

Fortunately, the vast majority of street crime is nonaggressive. However, there have been horror stories from travellers who underestimated the risk. The usual precautions apply: don't go down dodgy-looking streets and there is safety in numbers.

Remember that millions of people visit Barcelona each year and have nothing untoward happen to them – don't be put off, just be alert.

Lost Property

For the main lost property office (servei de troballes) call ☎ 93 402 31 61. For items that are lost on the metro call ☎ 93 318 70 74; at the airport call ☎ 93 298 33 49; or in a taxi call ☎ 93 223 40 12.

Keeping Copies

Make photocopies of all your important documents, keep some with you, separate from the originals, and leave a copy at home. You can also store details of documents in Lonely Planet's free online Travel Vault, which is password-protected and accessible worldwide. See e www.ekno.lonelyplanet.com.

Emergency Numbers

The EU standard emergency number is ☎ 112. Through this you can reach all emergency services (some operators are multi-lingual).

There are four different police forces in Barcelona but if you want to report a theft head to the *comisaría* (police station) of the Policía Nacional at C/Nou de la Rambla 80 (4, G3) where English is generally spoken and the staff are well versed in the likely scenario. For specific 24hr numbers call:

Ambulance *(Ambulància)*	☎ 061
Fire *(Bomberos)*	☎ 080
Municipal Police *(Policía Municipal)*	☎ 092
National Police *(Policía Nacional)*	☎ 091

Women Travellers

There is an indigenous problem with domestic violence against women in Spain but Barcelona shouldn't present any specific difficulties for female travellers. The vibe in the city is less macho than it once was and cases of harassment are few. That said, you should still exercise the same caution you would in any city and be careful which bars and clubs you frequent after dark (and especially when leaving them).

Information & Organisations

The Institut Català de la Dona (4, D6; C/de Portaferrissa 1-3, Barri Gòtic; ☎ 93 495 16 00) is the best all-round resource for women and can direct you to any service you require. The nationwide Comisión de Investigación de Malos Tratos a Mujeres (Commission of Investigation into the Abuse of Women) has a free 24hr national emergency line (☎ 900 10 00 09) although English is rarely spoken.

Gay & Lesbian Travellers

The growth in Barcelona's effervescent gay scene is matched only by the increase in tourist numbers. It's probably the gay capital of Spain and one of the pinkest cities in Europe. Gay and lesbian Catalan couples have been recognised by the state since 1988 and enjoy a range of rights, which stop just short of marital status. The community has considerable clout when it comes to the shaping of the city and is served by more than 200 establishments from bars and clubs to shops and saunas. Although they are dispersed throughout the city, the area of l'Eixample just beyond Universitat has such a concentration of gay venues that it has been dubbed 'Gaixample'. However, in keeping with the inclusive spirit of the city, the best places to go out and about aren't always the strictly gay ones.

Information & Organisations

The gay hotline (☎ 900 60 16 01; 6pm-10pm) is a useful resource and Casal Lambda at (4, H7; C/Ample 5, Barri Gòtic; ☎ 93 412 72 72) is a gay and lesbian social, cultural and information centre that also publishes a monthly magazine called LAMBDA. Coordinadora Gai-Lesbiana (2, H5; C/de Finlàndia 45, Sants; ☎ 93 298 00 29; e ccogailes@pangea.org) is the city council's coordinating body for gay and lesbian groups. Gay.com (e www.gay.com/index.html) and gaymap (e www.gaymap.ws/index .html) have useful information and links to Barcelona.

Entiendes and *Mensual* are both magazines with listings worth tracking down at gay bookshops (see p. 59), where you should also find a free handy map to gay Barcelona.

Senior Travellers

There are reduced prices for people aged over 60, 63 or 65 (depending on the place) at many attractions and occasionally on public transport. You usually have to show ID.

Disabled Travellers

Many older museums will pose problems if you're wheelchair-bound, while virtually all of the modern ones have adequate facilities. Some public transport (eg, metro line 2, some buses, taxis and the Aerobùs) is equipped but not to be relied upon. Call ☎ 93 486 07 52 for info on access points for public transport. Taxi Amic (☎ 93 358 11 11) is a reliable taxi company with mini-vans.

Look for the ♿ listed with individual reviews.

Information & Organisations

Contact the Institut Municipal de Persones amb Disminuciò (3, B9; C/de Llacuna 161, Sant Mart; ☎ 93 291 84 00) for details of facilities in the city. Two UK-based organisations, the Royal Association for Disability & Rehabilitation (RADAR; **e** www.radar.org.uk) and Holiday Care (**e** www.holidaycare.org.uk), may also be able to help if you contact them before you leave.

Language

Barcelona is a bilingual city, with both the local Catalan and Spanish (to be precise, Castilian – *castellano* to the Spanish) spoken by just about everyone. This section is based on Castilian. Where necessary, the masculine and feminine endings (usually 'o' and 'a' respectively) for words and phrases are given. For a more in-depth guide to the Spanish language, get a copy of Lonely Planet's *Spanish phrasebook*.

Basics

Hello.	*¡Hola!*
Goodbye.	*¡Adiós!*
Yes.	*Sí.*
No.	*No.*
Please.	*Por favor.*
Thank you.	*Gracias.*
You're welcome.	*De nada.*
Excuse me.	*Perdón/Perdone.*
Sorry/Excuse me.	*Lo siento/ Discúlpeme.*
Do you speak English?	*¿Habla inglés?*
I don't understand.	*No Entiendo.*
How much is it?	*¿Cuánto cuesta/vale?*

Getting Around

Where is (the metro station)?	*¿Dónde está (la parada de metro)?*
I want to go to ...	*Quiero ir a ...*
Can you show me (on the map)?	*¿Me puede indicar (en el mapa)?*
When does the ... leave/arrive?	*¿A qué hora sale/ llega el ...?*
bus	*autobús/bus*
train	*tren*
metro	*metro*
I'd like a ... ticket.	*Quisiera un billete ...*
one-way	*sencillo*
return	*de ida y vuelta*

Around Town

I'm looking for ...	*Estoy buscando ...*
a bank	*un banco*
the cathedral	*la catedral*
the hospital	*el hospital*
the old city	*la cuidad antigua*
the police	*la policía*
public toilets	*los aseos públicos*
a telephone	*un teléfono*
the tourist office	*la oficina de turismo*

Accommodation

Do you have any rooms available?	¿Tiene habitaciones libres?
a single room	una habitación individual
a double room	una habitación doble
a room with a bathroom	una habitación con baño
How much is it ...?	¿Cuánto cuesta ...?
per night	por noche
per person	por persona

Eating

breakfast	desayuno
lunch	almuerzo/comida
dinner	cena
I'd like the set menu.	Quisiera el menú del día.
Is service included?	¿El servicio está incluido?
I'm a vegetarian.	Soy vegetariano/a.

Time, Days & Numbers

What time is it?	¿Qué hora es?
today	hoy
tomorrow	mañana
yesterday	ayer
morning	mañana
afternoon	tarde
evening	noche
Monday	lunes
Tuesday	martes
Wednesday	miércoles
Thursday	jueves
Friday	viernes
Saturday	sábado
Sunday	domingo
0	cero
1	uno, una
2	dos
3	tres
4	cuatro
5	cinco
6	seis
7	siete
8	ocho
9	nueve
10	diez
100	cien/ciento
1000	mil

Health

I'm ...	Soy ...
diabetic	diabético/a
epileptic	epiléptico/a
asthmatic	asmático/a
I'm allergic to antibiotics penicillin	Soy alérgico/a a los antibióticos la penicilina

Emergencies

Help!	¡Socorro!/ ¡Auxilio!
Call ...	¡Llame a
a doctor!	un doctor!
the police!	la policía!
Where are the toilets?	¿Dónde están los servicios?
Go away!	¡Váyase!
I'm lost.	Estoy perdido/a.

Martin Hughes

View along Rambla de Catalunya with the Temple del Sagrat Cor in the background

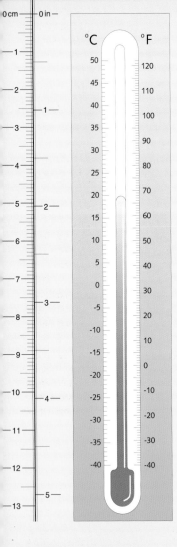

Conversion Tables

Clothing Sizes
Measurements approximate only; try before you buy.

Women's Clothing

Aust/NZ	8	10	12	14	16	18
Europe	36	38	40	42	44	46
Japan	5	7	9	11	13	15
UK	8	10	12	14	16	18
USA	6	8	10	12	14	16

Women's Shoes

Aust/NZ	5	6	7	8	9	10
Europe	35	36	37	38	39	40
France only	35	36	38	39	40	42
Japan	22	23	24	25	26	27
UK	3½	4½	5½	6½	7½	8½
USA	5	6	7	8	9	10

Men's Clothing

Aust/NZ	92	96	100	104	108	112
Europe	46	48	50	52	54	56
Japan	S		M	M		L
UK	35	36	37	38	39	40
USA	35	36	37	38	39	40

Men's Shirts (Collar Sizes)

Aust/NZ	38	39	40	41	42	43
Europe	38	39	40	41	42	43
Japan	38	39	40	41	42	43
UK	15	15½	16	16½	17	17½
USA	15	15½	16	16½	17	17½

Men's Shoes

Aust/NZ	7	8	9	10	11	12
Europe	41	42	43	44½	46	47
Japan	26	27	27.5	28	29	30
UK	7	8	9	10	11	12
USA	7½	8½	9½	10½	11½	12½

Weights & Measures

Weight
1kg = 2.2lb
1lb = 0.45kg
1g = 0.04oz
1oz = 28g

Volume
1 litre = 0.26 US gallons
1 US gallon = 3.8 litres
1 litre = 0.22 imperial gallons
1 imperial gallon = 4.55 litres

Length & Distance
1 inch = 2.54cm
1cm = 0.39 inches
1m = 3.3ft = 1.1yds
1ft = 0.3m
1km = 0.62 miles
1 mile = 1.6km

lonely planet

Lonely Planet is the world's most successful independent travel information company with offices in Australia, the US, the UK and France. With a reputation for comprehensive, reliable travel information and over 650 titles and 22 series catering for travellers' individual needs, Lonely Planet is a print and electronic publishing leader.

At Lonely Planet we believe that travellers can make a positive contribution to the countries they visit – if they respect their host communities and spend their money wisely. Since 1986 a percentage of the income from books has been donated to aid and human rights projects.

www.lonelyplanet.com

For news, views and free subscriptions to print and email newsletters plus a full list of LP titles, click on Lonely Planet's award-winning Web site.

On the Town

A romantic escape to Paris or a mad shopping dash through New York City, the locals' secret bars or a city's top attractions – whether you have 24 hours to kill or months to explore, Lonely Planet's On the Town products will give you the low-down.

Condensed guides are ideal pocket guides for when time is tight. Their quick-view maps, full-colour layout and opinionated reviews help short-term visitors target the top sights and discover the very best eating, shopping and entertainment options a city has to offer.

For more in-depth coverage, **city guides** offer insights into a city's character and cultural background as well as providing broad coverage of where to eat, stay and play. **CitySync**, a digital guide for your handheld unit, allows you to reference stacks of opinionated, well researched travel information. Portable and durable **city maps** are perfect for locating those back-street bars or hard-to-find local haunts.

'Ideal for a generation of fast movers.'

– *Gourmet Traveller* on Condensed guides

Condensed Guides

- Amsterdam
- Athens
- Bangkok (Sept 2002)
- Barcelona
- Boston
- Chicago
- Dublin
- Frankfurt
- Hong Kong
- London
- Los Angeles (Oct 2002)
- New York City
- Paris
- Prague
- Rome
- San Francisco (Oct 2002)
- Singapore (Oct 2002)
- Sydney
- Tokyo
- Venice (June 2002)
- Washington, DC

index

See also separate indexes for Places to Eat (p. 126), Places to Stay (p. 127), Shops (p. 127) and Sights with map references (p. 128).

PLACES TO EAT

PLACES TO STAY

SHOPS

sights – quick index